# Bad Dogs Have
# More Fun

# Bad Dogs Have More Fun

~ Selected Writings ~

on Family, Animals, and Life
by John Grogan
for *The Philadelphia Inquirer*

Vanguard Press
A Member of the Perseus Books Group

Hardcover edition first published in 2007 by Vanguard Books
Paperback edition first published in 2008 by Vanguard Books

The articles in this book were originally written by
John Grogan and published in a beloved column in
*The Philadelphia Inquirer*, which owns the rights to them.
This book is being published through an arrangement with
*The Philadelphia Inquirer*. Mr. Grogan has not participated
in its publication and is not profiting from it. A percentage
of profits from the sale of this book will go to The Good
Dog Foundation (www.thegooddogfoundation.org).

Set in 12 point Bembo

Cataloging-in-Publication data for this book is available
from the Library of Congress.
Hardcover ISBN: 978-1-59315-468-4
Paperback ISBN: 978-1-59315-490-5

Vanguard Press books are available at special discounts for
bulk purchases in the U.S. by corporations, institutions, and
other organizations. For more information, please contact the
Special Markets Department at the Perseus Books Group,
2300 Chestnut Street, Suite 200, Philadelphia, PA 19103,
or call (800) 810-4145, extension 5000, or e-mail
special.markets@perseusbooks.com.

10 9 8 7 6 5 4 3 2 1

# Contents

PART TWO

 *Animals*

PART THREE

*Life*

# Contents

# Family

## Deaf Girl Provides
## Lesson in Courage

Caitlin Reel was just six months old when her mother knew something was wrong.

The baby did not respond to voices or sounds, not even a loud clap of the hands. The doctors told Luann Reel not to worry. Her baby was fine.

But the mother persisted, and when doctors finally tested Caitlin's hearing a year later, they confirmed her fears.

Caitlin was living in a world of silence. She was profoundly deaf.

Flash forward ten years to last week at Shady Grove Elementary School in Ambler. The gymnasium was filled for the winter concert.

Music teacher Ryan Dankanich stepped to the microphone and told the audience they were about to hear "a very special violinist." The only clue he gave that this student had made a particularly arduous journey here was when he said, "Make sure you applaud very loudly."

And then out walked Caitlin, now 11, the deaf baby who never learned to give up. She lifted her violin to her chin and took a deep breath.

In the audience, Luann, the proud mom, stood poised with a video camera. Her hands were shaking.

"I was really worried," she said later from the family's home in Parkside in Delaware County. "She had crossed a lot of barriers to get here. I didn't want something really unpleasant to come out of her violin."

### A Long, Hard Battle

What a long road it had been. From birth, her daughter had been misunderstood, stared at, whispered about, incorrectly labeled—even by a teacher—as mentally retarded.

Caitlin set out to prove them wrong. She learned sign language and the rudiments of speech. She received a cochlear implant, which allows her to hear some sound. A major accomplishment came last fall when she ordered a Big Mac and fries all on her own.

While her hearing brother, Jared, 9, walks two blocks to school, Caitlin must ride 45 minutes or more each way. The Perm Delco School District buses her to Shady Grove Elementary, which has a program for hearing-impaired students run by the Montgomery County Intermediate Unit.

Caitlin saw hearing students arriving with musical instruments and said she wanted to play, too. And so, despite all odds, she began violin lessons—the first deaf child at the school to attempt them.

"It's taken a tremendous amount of concentration and perseverance on her part to get to this point," said Melanie Stefanatos, Caitlin's hearing-support teacher.

And last week's concert was her chance to show the world.

The audience hushed. Caitlin drew the bow across the strings. And out came . . . music. Slow, sweet, and steady— and with rock-solid timing. She played "Mary Had a Little Lamb" and "Twinkle, Twinkle Little Star."

Her mother fought back tears.

"I know she's not playing Tchaikovsky," Luann Reel, who is divorced, said. "But this is my deaf daughter—and she's playing the violin.

### An Incredible Feat

For most children, the brief performance would be just one of many Kodak moments on the road to adulthood. For Caitlin, it was a Herculean leap. To play this handful of notes, she had to overcome more obstacles than most of us will face in a lifetime.

As Dankanich, the music teacher, put it: "It's just an incredible feat she's been able to accomplish."

Caitlin probably will not go on to become a famous musician. She doesn't need to. The violin already has taught her about courage and perseverance and faith.

A girl without hearing tackled an instrument that has everything to do with hearing, and she didn't give up. For the determined, she learned, even the steepest mountains can be scaled, one step at a time.

Her performance over, Caitlin hurried off the stage. Principal Beth Pearson told the 500-member audience the truth about Caitlin—that she was one of the school's seven deaf children.

The audience roared its approval—loudly enough, in fact, that Caitlin could hear the clapping through her cochlear implant.

Backstage she signed to her mother: "I'm so happy. They were clapping for me. They were clapping for me."

*April 14, 2003*

# Food for Thought on Child-Rearing

The book arrived unannounced in plain brown paper.

On the cover was a photograph of a little girl beneath the title, *Too Much of a Good Thing: Raising Children of Character in an Indulgent Age.*

Hmmm. Was someone trying to tell me something?

A note inside solved the mystery. It was from an old high school friend who had done well enough financially to retire from his career as an investment adviser at the ripe old age of 45.

The way my investments have been going, I'll be working until I'm 95. Other than that, we have a lot in common.

We each have two boys and a girl of similar ages. We
each live in nice suburbs with good schools where most
children grow up assuming a God-given right to a minimum of 3,000 square feet of air-conditioned living space.

We each worry about what effect all this comfort will
have on our children. Nothing instills more dread in either of us than the S word. Spoiled.

And so he sent me the book with the caveat, "not that
you need this." Like heck I didn't. My idea of tough love
is saying no three times before caving in.

The book, by Harvard psychology professor Dan Kindlon, has been around for a couple of years and covers the
obvious bases: the perils of focusing on career over children,
on wealth over relationships, on indulgence instead of consequences.

Or as Kindlon put it, "Giving too much and expecting
too little."

### Breaking Bread

The book is filled with anecdotes of parents doing all the
wrong things to win their children's love—including hiring lawyers to help them avoid the consequences of their
bad actions. (Remember the student at Philadelphia's
Chestnut Hill Academy last fall whose parents hired a
lawyer to beat a deserved expulsion for secretly videotaping a female student?)

What makes this book different from the other parenting claptrap out there is its solid research. One fact
jumped out at me—the quantifiable correlation between
family meals and children who are blessedly normal.

Kindlon's research and a number of other national studies reach the same conclusion: Families that eat most meals together—and that means with Dad at the table—have children who are at a significantly lower risk for drug abuse, depression, promiscuity, and underachievement.

Easy enough. But I had to admit that work hours and long commutes had lately conspired to keep me away from the dinner table more times than not.

Last week, I found Kindlon at home in Boston during break in a publicity tour for his new book, *Tough Times, Strong Children*, and popped the question: Is it really that simple?

In a word, yes. Sitting down as a family, even if it is microwaved pizza, is a way to reconnect, share, and bond, Kindlon said. It lends structure and predictability and balances the negative influences of popular culture and wrong-track friends.

Hey, and you get to eat! I'm in.

### Fighting Back

"Basically, kids don't get in trouble as much when they are alone as when they are with friends," he said. "So when you allow the peer group to have more influence than the family, you're increasing your child's risk. Those family dinners are a time to remind the child: This is what we believe in, this is our view of the world."

But why dinner? Wouldn't, say, family walks do the same thing? Perhaps, but Kindlon suspects the food itself has a healing effect.

"Feeding kids, nurturing them—it's what parents do," the professor said. "There's something almost primordial about parents supplying food to their kids that cements the bond."

I also spoke with William Lessa, superintendent Hatboro-Horsham School District, who will speak tomorrow night at the Parenting Center at Abington on the importance of fathers.

Lessa agrees family meals are key.

"In our family, dinner was pretty much sacred," the father of two said. "Kids clearly need food. They also need guidance; they need structure; they need love." All of which can be provided around the dinner table.

So bring on the lasagna. Tonight, I swear, I'm wrapping up early and sitting down where I belong—at dinner with my family.

*April 21, 2003*

## Phila. in Spring, and Free Parking!

Some vacations just aren't meant to be. Our long-anticipated family spring break was one of them.

The plan was to drive to Williamsburg, Virginia, for five days of the kind of family togetherness you can achieve only by cramming five people into a standard hotel room. We would see the historic sites, eat in colonial taverns, buy tacky souvenirs, and swim at the hotel's indoor pool.

That was the plan.

A friendly little stomach bug known as rotavirus had other ideas. First it laid out my older son, then my daughter. Then my wife. Hey, gang! How's the vacation going so far?

According to the Centers for Disease Control and Prevention, rotavirus kills 600,000 children worldwide per year, mostly from dehydration brought on by relentless vomiting and diarrhea. In the United States, it lands 55,000 children in the hospital every year to receive intravenous fluids.

Two of them were my kids. It wasn't Busch Gardens, but the hospital did hand out free Easter baskets.

We stayed in denial for as long as possible, canceling our hotel reservations one night at a time.

By the weekend, with the patients resting comfortably in the Grogan Ebola Ward, my one remaining healthy child and I decided to salvage what little scrap of our derailed vacation we could. "Grab a jacket," I said. "We're going to Philadelphia."

### Been There, Done That

"You're not dragging me to the Liberty Bell again, are you?" my nine-year-old asked suspiciously. I shook my head no.

"Promise?"

"Promise."

And so we were off—with apples, water bottles, and bicycles.

By 10 a.m., we were parked off Kelly Drive. The day was as flawless as April days get, the air crisp, the cherry and pear trees in glorious bloom.

In Fairmount Park, we counted hawks and climbed rocks. Along the Schuylkill, we hung our feet over the water and waved to the rowing teams.

We pedaled north along the east bank of the river and then south again. You think driving on Interstate 95 is a death trap? Try the Kelly Drive bike path on a beautiful spring Sunday.

The whole city, it seemed, was on this path, enjoying the morning. We dodged speeding rollerbladers (an alarming number of them skating—this is not a misprint—backwards), strolling couples, darting toddlers, prancing dogs, and zipping cyclists.

Mostly, though, we dodged breathtakingly athletic, beautifully chiseled runners of every hue, every one of them with great teeth. To them I'd just like to say thanks for making me feel only slightly older than King Tut.

Eventually, we made our way to the Philadelphia Museum of Art, where a band was playing near the front steps.

"C'mon," I said, "Let's run up the stairs, just like in the movie."

"Uh, what movie?"

Oy. Kids nowadays—no culture.

## Up and Away

We ran up, anyway, me singing the *Rocky* theme song (now there's something no one's ever thought to try before), my son singing the "I've Got the Doofus Dad Humiliation Blues."

From the top, we gazed out over the urban skyline, this City of Brotherly Love newly dear to our hearts. I yelled the first thing that came to mind: "Hey! Come back with our bikes!"

Just kidding. The bikes, unchained and unattended, survived untouched.

We sat on the sidewalk and ate semi-petrified hot dogs that I'm pretty sure had been spinning on the rotisserie since before the Rizzo administration.

"Dad, these are the best hot dogs I've ever had!" the kid raved.

We stuck our heads inside dinosaur jaws at the Academy of Natural Sciences, marveled at the bathroom habits of the horses waiting to give carriage rides in the historic district, and traipsed through the Betsy Ross house, where it was all Dad could do not to crawl into the Widow Lithgow's bed and catch a few winks.

Best of all, we managed to nab free parking right on Arch Street. "Son," I said solemnly, "I want you to stop and reflect on this moment. It will likely never be repeated in your lifetime."

And so went our Philadelphia mini vacation. We came; we ate bad food; we avoided personal collisions—and no one got sick. All in all, not a bad way to spend a lovely spring day.

*June 10, 2003*

## A Refresher Course in Parenting 101

Good morning, class, and welcome to Parenting 101.

The purpose of this refresher course is to reinforce some of the basic skills we parents need to raise stable children who will grow up to be something other than residents of one of our fine local penitentiaries.

I apologize in advance if some of these points seem frightfully obvious. But a spate of parenting no-nos in recent months has shown that, when it comes to rearing children, it's best not to take anything for granted.

For instance, when in doubt, do not—I repeat, do not—punch out your son's Little League coach. I know all the other parents are doing it, but just keep telling yourself, "I am the role model. I am the role model."

When your 14-year-old has her classmates over for a sleepover, the proper question is not: "Do you kids take your margaritas with salt?"

Today's course uses actual news events from around our region to illustrate helpful parenting dos and don'ts. So let's get started.

Real news items: A 29-year-old woman was found guilty of leaving her 4-month-old son in the car while she shopped at a J.C. Penney store in Northeast Philadelphia. In Evesham, a 31-year-old woman was charged with leaving her two young children in a car for more than an hour while she was at a job interview.

Parenting 101 tip: Until Ford releases the Nannygate SUV, we suggest you take advantage of a little-known service available to parents in which trained individuals will actually come to your house and watch your children for a modest hourly fee. It's called baby-sitting.

Real news item: A father and his 19-year-old son were arrested in West Chester after a chase and charged with a string of home burglaries.

Parenting 101 tip: When we stressed the need for father-son bonding opportunities, we more had in mind touch football and weekend fishing trips.

Real news items: A Southwest Philadelphia woman was charged with placing duct tape over her 7-month-old son's mouth because he was crying too much. In a separate case, a Bucks County woman was charged with wrapping two foster children and a biological child in duct tape, and her estranged husband was charged with photographing the bound children.

Parenting 101 tip: Yes, it's true that children need certain constraints in their lives. And it's true that duct tape has many useful purposes around the house. But let's keep those two thoughts separate.

Real news items: Police said a 7-year-old girl steered the family auto down the Blue Route last year at speeds ranging from 5 to 50 mph, while her drunken mother worked the brake and gas pedals.

Parenting 101 tip: When we said "designated driver," we were thinking of someone old enough to see over the dashboard. Ever hear of a taxi, lady?

Real news item: Ebony Smith, 10, of Philadelphia, was released from the hospital last month after she was shot in the head in February following a snowball fight. Arrested in the drive-by shooting was the mother of another girl who was hit by a snowball, and the woman's fiancé.

Parenting 101 tip: I'm not sure what's scarier, the right to bear arms or the right to bear children. Put them together and you have a good argument for licensing both.

Real news item: A Fort Washington woman is awaiting trial on charges that she embezzled $65,000 from the Horsham Hawks during her tenure as the youth football league's treasurer. Her husband was convicted of slugging another parent, the Hawks' president, in the nose during a confrontation about the missing money.

Parenting 101 tip: While we laud the spirit of volunteerism, in this case, we must point out that draining the college fund is a more efficient way of stealing from your children. And, dads, Mike Tyson is probably not the best model for resolving disputes.

Finally, we here at Parenting 101 have received several reports of parents buying alcohol, condoms, and motel rooms for their underage children.

(All in good fun, right?)

Mom and Dad, we know you want to be the coolest parents in the PTA. But sometimes a grown-up just has to say no. Bummer, huh?

Now get out there and give it a try.

Class dismissed.

*August 29, 2003*

## Girl, 4, Offers Hope
## by Way She Lived

At Our Lady of Mount Carmel Church in Doylestown yesterday, a small white casket sat at the edge of the altar, its lid opened to show the frail body of a young fighter.

Her name was Katie Ann Duffin, and she would have turned 5 this week. Instead, about 300 people gathered on a lovely summer's day to say goodbye to this little girl

who faced down cancer with a bravery and optimism sel-
dom seen in anyone of any age.

All morning long, the people came. They filed past in a
long, slow procession, each one greeted with a hug from
Katie's parents, Paul and Terry Duffin of Doylestown.
Many who came had known the girl. Others had never
met her but felt they somehow knew her, too.

It was because of her Web site, www.katieduffin.com,
which faithfully chronicled in weekly journal entries her
long battle against what she called the blob growing inside her.

The Web site was written in her voice by her uncle,
Hugh Saunders, to capture her fighting spirit. It started as
a way to keep friends abreast of her medical progress, but
it grew into something bigger. From across the country,
countless strangers logged on to follow her struggle to
survive, many of them leaving her messages of support in
her online guest book.

Her story begins six months after her birth on August 23,
1998, when doctors discovered a golf-ball-size malignancy
beneath her left shoulder. They operated twice and subjected her to six rounds of chemotherapy. As Katie's journal
states, "All was great until four years later, almost to the day."

In March, the blob returned. And this time it had long
tentacles that reached up along her spine. And that's
where Katie's weekly entries begin:

March 11: "The doctors told us that the golf-ball thing
is back again near my shoulder and neck. . . . They decided that they would have two operations, one from the
back and one from the front."

March 22: "I am feeling OK and even asked my mom if I could go to school yesterday. It took a little convincing but she let me go. I had a great time. I am not going to let this thing slow me down."

April 6: "Tomorrow is the big day. The doctors will be giving me that 'funny juice' again to make me go to sleep so they can go in and get the rest of the golf ball out of my shoulder."

April 7: "Great news! . . . Dr. Greg just came in and told my mom and dad that the [spinal] fluid is clear—no bad cells in my spine. I think this time mom and dad were crying because they were happy, and that makes me happy."

And so the entries go, swaying from the dire to the mundane, through surgeries and radiation treatments and chemotherapy and nausea and morphine drips. And always there is Katie's voice, the voice of a little fighter unwilling to throw in the towel.

May 23: "I told [the doctor] he is not dealing with the ordinary patient. I am Katie Duffin, a mean lean fighting machine."

But by early July, Katie was unable to keep food down and was put on a feeding tube. She was dogged by constant headaches. And in mid-July came very bad news: The malignancy had spread to her brain. "OK, guys, now is the time to really rally the troops and give me as many prayers as you can muster," one entry states.

July 21, the final entry written in her voice: "I am definitely hanging in there."

The last entry, signed by her parents and older brother, Paul Jr., was logged August 12: "Hello everyone. This is the update that we knew was coming but we never wanted to write. Today at 9:30 p.m., Katie finally allowed the angel to take her hand and show her the way to heaven."

At yesterday's Funeral Mass, the Rev. Charles Hagan noted that this remarkable girl's short life "touched so many thousands of people," many of them through her Web site. And to each she offered a message.

"She never, ever, ever gave up hope," the priest said. "This is her legacy to us."

*September 19, 2003*

# A Friendship Born
# of Two Mothers' Grief

Dateline: SHANKSVILLE, Pennsylvania.

As I stood last week overlooking the hillside near this tiny western Pennsylvania farm town where Flight 93 crashed two years ago, I was drawn to a sun-bleached photograph.

It hung from one of the 40 painted angels planted here to memorialize each of the passengers and crew who died that day. The photo shows an attractive woman with lustrous dark hair, bright eyes, and a carefree smile.

Her name was Honor Elizabeth Wainio. She was 27, a rising regional manager for Discovery Channel stores in

Watchung, New Jersey. And she had been on her way to a business meeting in San Francisco when her life ended in this field at 10:06 a.m. on September 11, 2001.

As I contemplated this young life cut short, an older woman stepped up and placed a red rose beneath the photo. She stood there a long time.

When the woman turned to leave, I asked, "Did you know her?"

She thought for a moment, then said: "Not exactly. Not while she was alive."

And thus began one of the countless untold stories that continue to rise from the ashes of the 9/11 tragedy.

It is the story of two mothers from very different worlds—one a rural Christian farm wife, the other an urban Jewish professional—finding solace and dear friendship in shared grief.

### A Snowstorm and Death

The woman with the rose, I learned, is Shirley Hillegass, a grandmother who lives with her husband, Robert, on 245 verdant acres of corn and hay about three miles from the crash site.

During a treacherous snowstorm in 1994, her daughter, Annette, 32, was killed in a car crash.

Hillegass thought she had boxed up her sorrow as much as a mother could. "You don't ever get over the loss," she said. "You just learn to accept the fact that this is the way it is; this is the way it will always be."

Then came the terrorist attacks, and she found the wound wide open again. One victim in particular touched her. It was Elizabeth Wainio, the young woman in the photograph.

She seemed like Annette in so many ways. Both were vivacious, ambitious, so full of life.

Six months after the attack, at a memorial service in Shanksville for which virtually the whole town turned out, Hillegass, as chance would have it, found herself sitting behind Wainio's stepmother, Esther Heymann, a one-time banker from Baltimore.

"I can't explain it. I'm normally not someone to speak to a stranger," Hillegass said. "I just did what my heart told me I had to do. I don't know if it was an angel or Annette saying, 'Mom, you need to reach out to that woman.'"

So, after the service, she summoned her nerve and introduced herself.

### "I Love You, Mom"

Heymann, who married Wainio's father when the girl was 5 and loved her as her own, was who Wainio called by Airfone in the minutes before the doomed plane crashed. She was the one to hear her stepdaughter's final words: "They're getting ready to break into the cockpit. I have to go. I love you, Mom. Good-bye."

In the months that followed, those words hung like unbearable weights around Heymann's neck. Into that all-consuming grief stepped another mother, a self-described "country hick," who understood it first-hand.

Heymann said she was leery of strangers trying to befriend her after the crash. But Hillegass was somehow different. "I had an instinct about this woman's genuineness," she said. "I just knew she was very special."

The friendship began cautiously with a few respectful words followed by letters and phone calls. Over the months, the women have bonded like sisters. A week ago today, the day after the second anniversary of that awful morning, they met at Hillegass's farmhouse near the crash site to hug, exchange small gifts, and simply talk.

"I don't know if I literally believe in angels, but I know there are a lot of people walking around on earth who are angels," Heymann said. "And Shirley is one of them."

For her part, Hillegass said the healing has been mutual. "She's helped me as much as I've helped her," she said.

Two daughters. Two deaths. Two mothers bonded in grief. And, slowly, together, a dawning realization that for the living, life goes on.

*December 23, 2003*

# A Wish
## *One More Magic Christmas*

A few days ago as I hung holiday decorations, my daughter asked, "Daddy, is Santa really real?"

Her two older brothers had been filling her head with doubts again. "Do you believe he's real?" I asked, stalling. She nodded vigorously, blonde bangs bouncing up and down.

"Then he must be real," I said. And that reassurance, lame as it was, seemed to suffice. She informed me she would be putting out four cookies this year instead of the customary three because Santa had emptied the plate last Christmas. Then she skipped happily off to write him a letter.

Colleen is 6, in first grade, our youngest child—and somehow no longer a baby. If I had any say in the matter, I'd still be feeding her warm bottles and counting my success by the velocity of her burps.

But in this I have no say.

She is moving from the nest like an ocean liner moves from the dock, slowly but with unstoppable momentum. Tug on the mooring lines all you want; it will do no good. On the horizon, adulthood beckons.

Her older brothers, 11 and 10, have moved through the same stages before her. But because she is our last, the passage is all the more bittersweet. All I can say is thank god for video cameras.

With each hurdle she leaps, another chapter in that book called childhood closes forever. Like any good book, I don't want it to end.

## Last Stop: Goodwill

As she reaches each benchmark—first step, first word, first school day—my wife and I at once cheer and sigh. We capture the moment on tape and try to ignore those little stabbing pangs of loss.

Last spring, Colleen decided she was done with training wheels. I removed them from her bike and spent the weekend running up and down our street beside her, holding her by the seat as she fought for balance. Out of sheer exhaustion, I finally let go—and was amazed, and just a little sad, to see her ride down the block without me, not once looking back.

When her big brothers mastered bicycles, the training wheels went to the next in line. But this time they went to Goodwill. That era of our lives is over.

It was the same for the stroller and the crib and the booster seat, all rendered obsolete seemingly overnight, reminders of how quickly babies grow to children and children grow to teenagers and teenagers leave home.

The day she learned to say "John" instead of "Wahn" nearly broke my heart.

I try not to be too sentimental about these things. Spring turns to summer, kids grow up. Believe me, the day I changed my final diaper will go down as one of the unequivocally happiest of my life. What can I say? Some stages are easier to let go of than others. You can imagine how broken up I am that no one screams to watch Barney anymore.

I'm counting the years until I can get one of those "I'm spending my kids' inheritance" bumper stickers.

## The Art of Letting Go

And yet.

Parents are meant to prepare their children for the outside world, to make them strong and independent. So why am I feeling left out because no one needs me to tie shoes anymore?

I mentioned this to a woman friend of mine, and she asked, "So men have those feelings, too?" Yeah, I guess sometimes we do, at least when there's nothing good on ESPN.

My friend Joe Schwerdt, a father of three boys, confessed to feeling the same tug. His youngest, Andrew, is the family's last to play Little League, and father and son have been practicing. But each toss of the ball carries a reminder of what soon will pass. "He's my last boy and I'm hanging onto his childhood as long as I can," my friend wrote me. "I fear on the day he turns 13 he'll suddenly discover the generation gap, put his baseball glove away, and put on a pair of headphones."

This holiday I want just one gift. And that is for my youngest to squeeze a final magic Christmas out of her childhood—to have one more year of wonderment, of believing in jolly elves and prancing reindeer with no other purpose in life but to spread generosity and joy.

Come Christmas morning, I will be up before dawn, video camera in hand, to capture my daughter's face as she races to check the plate of cookies. I'm betting Santa will have eaten every last one.

*March 1, 2004*

# For Teen Mother,
# the Son Is Rising

In her low-slung jeans and powder-blue sneakers, Kate Gowen could be any high school senior—except for one small detail. On her lap sits a 7-month-old baby boy.

His name is Donovan, named after the quarterback. The one-time North Penn High School student became pregnant with him shortly after she turned 16. And now, not quite a year and a half later, she realizes her carefree— and, she admits, wild—childhood is officially behind her.

Yet she tells you this baby in all likelihood saved her life, literally—from jail, a drug overdose, or worse. And given her self-destructive path before his birth, you can believe it.

Sitting with Donovan in the small apartment in Hatfield that she shares with her mother, Kate admits she was about as difficult as teenagers come. Starting at age 14, she tried just about everything.

She disappeared overnight, stole her mother's car, ran away from home, skipped school for weeks at a time, experimented with alcohol and drugs, and became sexually active.

"I was a total pothead," she says. "I fell in with a group of kids. We had this 'the world is against us' mentality."

She threatened suicide several times and ended up in the mental-health system. "I never wanted to die," she now says, "but it was a real attention grabber."

Her mother, a single parent working as a waitress and dealing with her own personal problems, was unable to control the girl. "She was very angry," Laura Gowen said.

By age 15, Kate found herself in an alternative school for troubled teens. She lasted two months before pulling a knife on a student, getting expelled and hauled into Montgomery County juvenile court. A judge placed her on home probation. Within hours she had run away again, and this time the judge locked her up for 22 days.

Kate, a thin girl with long dark hair and pretty eyes, is not sure why she was so angry. She had never known her father, but her childhood in the suburbs was otherwise fully ordinary.

"I just had this image of myself as this hardened, tough girl," she says.

On Halloween 2002, a month after her 16th birthday, she learned she was pregnant. After three anguished weeks, with nearly everyone she knew urging her to have an abortion, Kate made her decision.

"I just couldn't live with terminating this pregnancy," she said. "And I couldn't see myself carrying him for nine months and then just giving him up. So I decided to keep him."

The pregnancy landed her at a place that she says profoundly changed her life for the better—the Lakeside Pregnancy and Parenting Center, a nonprofit, private school for teenage mothers in Fort Washington.

It was small, just 30 students, and the counselors and teachers worked intensely with her. They showered her with attention, teaching life skills, driving her to doctor's appointments, and pushing her academically.

Mostly, they just believed in her.

"Kate is very bright," Nancy Kane, the school's director, told me. "As far as IQ, she is a gifted kid."

Since Donovan's birth in July, Kate has made a "huge turnaround," Kane said, and thrown herself into parenting and schoolwork. Once considered at high risk for dropping out, she is back on track to graduate with her North Penn classmates in June.

Kate says she has been sober since the day she learned she was pregnant, and she is proud that she delivered a healthy, 9-pound baby.

She says she avoids her old crowd and finds friendship now in the other young moms she has met. After graduation, she plans to pursue nursing.

Life won't be easy, but it has a new purpose. And a joy, as well.

"My son is the driving force in my life," she says. "He's everything. He's helped me turn from a melodramatic teenager headed to a grave or a jail cell into someone worth respecting."

She lifts him over her head and adds: "I owe everything to him, and I'm working my hardest to give him the wonderful life he deserves."

*April 12, 2004*

## Mother Keeps the Passion Alive

Christine Detwiler, teacher and mother, stands before a group of students at North Penn High School near Lansdale and tries to explain why she is putting up $100 of her own money as a prize for an essay contest.

You see, she tells them, "My son, Ben, was once a student here, too." And then she adds in a calm, even voice she has had 13 years to practice: "He died when he was a junior."

It was the night of October 26, 1991, and Ben, 16, and a friend were walking home along Route 309 from the Montgomery Mall in North Wales, where Ben worked baking cinnamon rolls.

The distance was less than a mile, and the boys were walking in the grass, neither of which made any difference in the end. A drunken driver veered off the road, killing Ben instantly. She was convicted and sentenced to three years in prison.

Life is filled with little ironies. And one that will always haunt Ben's mother is the fact that she would not permit Ben to drive until he was 18, figuring she could keep him safe that way.

Detwiler, an elementary school teacher in the North Penn district, mentions none of this to the students before her. Rather, she tells them what kind of a boy her son was—an idealist, an activist, a thinker, and a talker who loved to debate issues.

"He was also a pretty good writer," she tells the students.

### A Better World

And that is why, shortly after his death, seeking some positive outlet in which to pour her bottomless grief, she established the Ben Detwiler Writing Contest for juniors at the school. Ben once wrote that his goal was to make the world a better place, and that is the theme for the contest, now in its 13th year.

She continues to sponsor the event, Detwiler later told me, as a way of keeping her son's memory alive—a way of holding on to him for just a little longer. "I want young people to do the active thinking about their world that Ben can no longer do," she said.

Ben, she tells you, was the kind of kid who navigated adolescence outside the mainstream. He was small for his age and not athletic, and by the time he reached high school he was cultivating a punk-rock appearance, dyeing his hair black and wearing it in a spiked Mohawk cut. He pierced his nose, wore black leather, and played guitar in a rock band.

Because of his look, many students and parents assumed he was trouble best avoided. Being ostracized by some taught him early lessons about prejudice and stereotypes. It also led him into an unexpected friendship with an unlikely ally, the school's principal, Juan Baughn, an African American who himself knew the sting of being outside the majority. The two spent many hours after school talking and debating—and, Baughn points out, coming to respect each other.

## A Shared Pain

"It hurt him, the disapproval," said Baughn, who is now an assistant schools superintendent in Washington, DC. "It just blew him away that people were not more receptive to who he was inside instead of just what he looked like. At one point, Ben said to me, 'Dr. Baughn, you know what it's like?' And I did, and I do."

The former principal was happy to hear Ben's mother has kept the essay contest going. "He was a little guy with a great big heart," Baughn said. "He wanted to save the world. I kept talking to him about saving his piece of it."

And so again this year, a group of North Penn juniors who were just toddlers when Ben died will try their hand at capturing that same passion.

They will write about war and poverty and, perhaps, about accepting those who don't look like they do.

The winner will take home a plaque and a check. And the mother, if she is lucky, might catch a glimpse of her son in their words.

His classmates are adults now, with careers and marriages and kids of their own. They have moved on, and so has Ben's mother, as best she can.

But a part of her remains frozen in the fall of her son's junior year. That's how she sees him still, a vulnerable teen with a great big heart, searching for his place in this world.

"Right now he would be 29," she says in that voice of hers, the calluses of time cushioning a mother's grief. "I have a son who will always be 16."

_July 13, 2004_

## Getaway Becomes Dad–Son Mind Trip

A 12-year-old mind is a strange and beautiful thing to behold.

And when I drove into the dawn with my son recently for a four-day backpacking trip in the Allegheny National Forest, I got to behold more than I would wish on any parent. There was no mom, no little brother or sister. Only the two of us.

The kid just would not shut up.

To help pass the six-hour drive, I had brought along a large supply of favorite tunes—my music, not his, of course. But he kept turning down the volume so he could chat my ear off.

"You just turned down Jimi Hendrix," I admonished. "Don't you know it's a sin to turn down Jimi Hendrix?"

"Dad, you always play it too loud."

"That's not possible," I retorted.

He eased the volume down. There were questions galore that needed answering.

"Hey, Dad, if Mars veered off course and crashed into Earth, what do you think would happen?"

"That's impossible," I said.

"But what if it wasn't? Then what?"

"I have no idea," I said, "but I'm pretty sure you'd use it as an excuse to get out of doing homework."

Next question: "If you had to eat poison, what kind would you pick?"

"I would never eat poison—and neither should you."

"But let's just say you had to."

I refused to answer on the grounds that no father should be endorsing toxic substances. But he wouldn't relent. "I don't know," I finally said. "Hemlock?" I figured if it worked for Socrates, it worked for me.

### Weird and Evil

"What's the weirdest thing ever?"

"You?"

"That's not funny." Two-second pause, and then: "Who's the most evil person in all of history?"

"Easy," I said.

"And it can't be Hitler."

"I was going to say Hitler."

"Everyone says Hitler. That's too easy. Someone other than Hitler."

And so went the long drive. I was tempted to duct-tape the boy's mouth shut—a disciplinary measure for which there is ample precedent here in our region. And I just might have tried it, except for this one thing: He's 12 and still thinks his father holds the answers to all mysteries. Next year he will be 13, officially a teenager, and things no doubt will be different.

By 13, he'll consider me somewhere between mold spores and pond scum on the spectrum of valued information sources. I thought I'd better enjoy the babble while I could. He's talking now, I told myself, let him. Soon enough he just might go silent, and then I'd be kicking myself.

So I rolled down the windows to breathe in the country smells of mowed hay and cow manure and let the inquisition continue.

His mind was a preadolescent cauldron of popping, snapping, crackling synapses, and it jumped all over as he chased his curiosity.

What was the worst disaster? The biggest crime? Coolest invention?

### Politics and Presidents

"Who's your favorite Republican?"

"Ever?"

"Ever."

"Abraham Lincoln."

"Favorite Democrat?" he asked.

"Harry Truman."

"Who's the most famous person you've ever met?"

"Frank Zappa."

"Who's he?"

"Oy. Kids nowadays."

"Who else who's famous?"

"I interviewed the first George Bush once," I said.

"Really? Was he nice?"

"Very nice."

"Were you nervous?" he asked.

"Just a little."

"Too cool," he said.

The questions and answers continued through our hike deep into the woods, through dinner on a ledge overlooking a fast-moving brook, and through the fire's dying embers.

I was beat, but I dared not stop him, knowing in a year, or perhaps even a month, he would be cringing at his father's glory-days' tales of close encounters with dead rock stars and past presidents. For now he was all ears, and I was too cool. I'd take it.

As the moon rose over the trees, I finally managed to get in a question of my own. "So, kiddo," I asked. "What do you say we go to sleep now?"

## Brain-Damaged but Still a "Gift"

Her name is Millie.

She came into this world 55 years ago, a healthy, chubby baby with a shock of dark hair. Her family loved her then, and despite everything—or perhaps because of it—loves her now even more.

Millie Reynolds has never spoken a word or returned a smile. Her first tentative baby steps would be her last. Just before her first birthday in 1950, she contracted viral meningitis, with sustained fevers that left her profoundly brain-damaged.

The doctors said an institution would be best, but Millie's parents would not listen. They brought their damaged baby home to the Olney section of Philadelphia and lovingly cared for her as she grew, unaware, from a child to an adolescent to an adult.

Today her world is a small bedroom on the second floor of the Cheltenham home of her older brother, Charles Reynolds, and his wife, Susan, who took over Millie's 24/7 care after the parents' deaths. For the last 17 years, the couple have dedicated their lives to her without regret.

"She is our forever baby," Susan Reynolds says, gazing upon Millie lying wide-eyed but unseeing beneath a picture of Jesus. And Millie is.

She requires diapers and total care. Until four years ago, when a feeding tube was surgically inserted as her swallowing reflex weakened, she sucked milk from a bottle and was spoon-fed pureed fruits and vegetables.

## A Child's Face

She is blind, and paralyzed from the neck down. Her hands curl up against her wrists, and her spine over the years has taken the shape of a curving mountain road. She weighs just 80 pounds, and with her soft skin and black hair not showing a strand of gray, she looks almost like a teenager, even a child.

Ask her family whether Millie's life has value or meaning, if the kindest course might not be to simply remove the feeding tube so she can escape the prison of her broken body, and they just smile.

"Millie is a gift," Susan Reynolds, a third-grade teacher, says. "Her life has brought many blessings to our family."

Adds her husband, a furniture salesman: "She has taught us the importance of life."

The couple are devout Catholics, and caring for Millie has cemented their conviction that all life, even one as compromised as this, is precious.

They say Millie has taught them charity, patience, and unqualified love. She has shown them what really matters in life. Most important, they say, her continual presence has given their three now-grown children the greatest gift of all—compassion.

Not bad for a human life many would dismiss as better off dead.

In exchange, they give her loving, dignified care. They point out proudly that Millie's doctors are in awe that she has never suffered a single bedsore in 54 years.

### Who Decides?

The Reynoldses have followed with interest—and dismay—the national uproar over Terri Schiavo, the brain-damaged former Huntingdon Valley woman whose feeding tube, a judge ruled last week, could be removed as early as March 18.

What is missing from the debate, they believe, is a simple but fundamental question: Whose right is it, anyway, to decide what constitutes a life worth living? Can any human really make that decision about another?

The Reynoldses believe not.

Despite what some medical ethicists say, they do not see Millie's feeding tube as an artificial means to prolong life but simply as a medical tool to allow her to more comfortably and safely get the sustenance all humans need. Before the tube, she had aspirated food into her lungs, leading to critical bouts of pneumonia.

When Millie's time comes—and she grows weaker each year—they will not order any extraordinary measures to prolong life. But neither will they ever consider steps to shorten it. That decision, they believe, is between Millie and a higher authority.

"Our faith and our love, that's what has guided us," Susan Reynolds says.

As she talks, her forever baby rocks her head from side to side, her tongue out slightly, her sightless gaze far away in that netherworld the rest of us will never comprehend, somewhere between here and forever gone.

## Speeder Dad Learns
## an Important Lesson

It was one of those amazing spring days that demand a drive in the country. The sun was brilliant, the sky a cloudless blue, the earth's awakening smell sweet on the air.

"Hop in," I told the kids. "We're taking a ride." A ride to nowhere and for no purpose other than to feel the wind in our faces and to take in the eye-popping beauty of budding maples and blossoming cherry trees.

We found our way to one of those bucolic Bucks County country roads that artists draw. We whizzed past cows and barns and pastures, the sunroof open, the windows down, and Stevie Wonder on the stereo. Bliss.

Then I glanced in my rearview mirror. Bliss be gone.

A police car was tight on my tail, lights flashing, siren wailing. A choice swear word nearly escaped my lips before I remembered the kids and uttered, "Shoot. Golldarnitall!"

With sinking heart, I pulled over, knowing I had been having way too much fun not to have been speeding. But the cop whizzed by me, instead pulling over the pickup truck I had been following. Whew, better him than me, I thought.

My good fortune was short lived. The state trooper, it turned out, was going for a double play. He waved me over behind the pickup. I handed him my driver's license.

"Mr. Grogan, are you in a hurry today?" he asked.

"Actually, no," I said.

## No Good Excuses

I wanted to tell him about the joyous riot of spring, the blue sky, the budding trees, the awakening earth, and all that. I wanted to extol the wind in my face and the unadulterated pleasure of Stevie Wonder and an open sunroof on a day so perfect—neither too hot nor too cold—it could have been delivered by angels. But I was pretty sure the *joie de vivre* defense was not going to cut it.

"You were driving 62 in a 40-mph zone," he told me. And then he delivered the most withering blow of all: "And with children in the car!"

His tone was a cross of contempt and concern, and the words stung. What kind of a father would go speeding around curves with his own flesh-and-blood beside him? The only good news was that the guy in the pickup had been going ever faster—and he had his kid along, too.

The punishment for my lead-footed indiscretion: a $160 fine and three points on my driving record. But that was nothing compared to what awaited me when I glanced at the face of my 8-year-old daughter in the backseat. My son, 12, was more amused than anything by my predicament. But Colleen looked stricken.

I was her dad. And to a second grader, that meant I was her hero, her compass, her rock of stability and righteousness. I was the one who kept her safe, who always told her the police were there to protect her from bad people.

I was the guy who regularly admonished her to obey the rules and do the right thing, even when no one was watching.

And here I was, caught red-handed on the wrong side of the law.

### Off the Pedestal

Yes, it was only a speeding ticket, but I could see it on her face, the dawning awareness that her father was less than perfect, was in fact something approaching criminal.

The trooper seemed to see it, too, and in a softer tone said, "We're just trying to keep everyone safe."

And then to Colleen: "I'm glad to see you all wearing your seatbelts."

Her face brightened. See, her dad wasn't a total bum!

I thanked the officer—why, I'm not quite sure—and drove off with all the zip of a church lady on her way to Sunday services.

I have preached ad nauseam to my kids that actions have consequences, and now I was Exhibit A.

"I learned an important lesson today," I told them. "The rules are there for a reason, and I broke them, and now I have to pay."

It's odd, this family affair. We spend the first half of our lives hiding our imperfections from our parents so as not to disappoint them, and we spend the second half hiding them from our children for the same reason.

On this achingly lovely day, I had no place to hide. My little game was up.

Speeder Dad was guilty as charged.

## Introducing a Gift Named Danny

Friday was the day Susan Haggerty had apprehensively awaited for weeks. Her coming-out day.

Nerves on edge, she walked into her son Jack's fourth-grade class at St. Alphonsus in Maple Glen, Montgomery County. Jack greeted his mother at the door and then returned to his seat, surrounded by his classmates.

He, too, was ready for this moment. Some teasing had begun. Some things had been said. It was time.

His mother paused in front of the class, took a breath and then said: "Jack has a brother. Jack's brother has autism."

There. It was said.

Not that Haggerty had hidden the fact, but some things are harder to talk about than others. This was her first time standing before a group of this size to disclose her son's autism.

She asked the children whether they knew what that word meant, and one bespectacled girl shot up her hand and said, "It's like you're kind of out of control sometimes."

"They have a problem with their brains," said another.

"You've been reading up!" the mother praised her.

In simple sentences, she told Danny's story. He was a beautiful newborn, perfect in every way. But his parents began to notice he was not like the other babies. He did not cry like they did, did not chatter, did not achieve the same milestones.

## Different Drummers

In 1998, when Danny was 2, the parents received the formal diagnosis.

What she wanted the students to know is that children such as Danny, while different, are not to be feared. Sometimes they grunt; sometimes they flap their arms or get right in your face. They have a hard time looking in your eyes. But they mean no harm.

"If you're not afraid of them, you might find out they're nice guys," she tells the children, "They want to have friends, too."

This coming out as an autism parent is not meant just for the children, but for their parents, too. She gives each child a two-page letter to take home. In it, Haggerty bares her soul.

"We had the usual expectations and dreams that parents have for their children," she wrote. "On this particular day [when Danny was diagnosed], everything in the world changed for my husband and me."

And she told them something else—that Danny is not the only one in their home with autism. His younger brother, Will, 7, has been diagnosed with a milder form of the condition.

She apologized if her children disturb anyone at Sunday Mass. "We want you to know how much we appreciate your patience and kindness," she concluded.

## Separate and Apart

After Haggerty finished her talk, as the children streamed out of class, she confessed that life as the parent of autistic children can be lonely and isolated. The invitations to socialize are painfully few, she said, adding, "I've learned to grow a tougher skin."

But she and her husband now know what really matters, and most of it exists within the four walls of a family's home.

She has discovered that sometimes amazing gifts come in surprising packages. Sometimes they are wrapped in heartbreak.

Before Friday's presentation at St. Alphonsus, Haggerty took me to another school a few blocks away, Maple Glen Elementary, where I met the gift that is Danny.

He charged into the room, arms aflutter, eyes darting, and smashed his lips against his mother's.

He is a beautiful, freckle-faced boy with watery blue eyes who speaks in two- and three-word sentences, which makes his mother beam with pride. Just months ago, he was limited to one-word responses.

Thinking he is going home, he says, "I get backpack. My tummy rumbles."

He cannot tell me his age—nine, but he knows what he will do when he gets home. It's the same thing he does every day

"Rewind!" he squeals.

And that is what he literally will do, over and over again: rewind videotapes, their soothing whir comforting him. His mother laughs, hugs him. He prances off like a stallion.

Jack's brothers have autism. This family is through apologizing.

## When a Child Goes Missing

It had the makings of every parent's worst nightmare—a missing child.

My best friend from college was visiting with his wife and two daughters. I loaded them and my three children into the minivan for a tour of historic Bethlehem. One second we were nosing our way through colonial-era ruins along a fast-moving river; the next I was yelling, "Where's Conor?"

My middle child, who was 7 at the time, had simply disappeared. "He was just here a second ago," my friend Pete Kelly said.

His wife, Maureen, gathered up the other children, and Pete and I searched the area. As the minutes ticked by, I focused ever more frantically on two scenarios. One involved the icy river with its rapids and jagged boulders; the other involved a man who had been playing with a puppy nearby and now was gone, too.

Pete, a police officer in Michigan, seemed to be having the same thoughts. I trotted along the riverbank, peering with dread into the water; he dodged in and out of old foundations and buildings, anywhere someone could pull a child.

After 20 minutes, we met up again. "Nothing," he said.

I looked at him, not wanting to say what I was thinking. He was the cop; I trusted his judgment.

"I think it's time to call 911," he said.

He ran to a store to find a phone; I returned to the stream. Two minutes later, I heard his shouts from a block away, and when I turned, he held my son above his head.

### Relief and Gratitude

Relief, so intense I felt my legs wobble, washed over me.

Conor had wandered out of sight, and when he couldn't find us he did exactly what I had taught him to do: He returned to the car to wait for us. There he was when Pete reached the street, sitting on the curb, bravely fighting back tears.

If only the family of Jamil Guy could have had such a happy ending.

The 13-year-old drowned in Chester Creek on Monday after he and his two cousins tried to turn a small, plastic wading pool into a boat.

They were supposed to be at their grandmother's house, but they had sneaked down to the creek across from Chester High School. They were boys being boys. Boys doing what boys have always done and always will.

Jamil Guy's death stopped me short and made me appreciate my lucky draw. It reminded me how differently my own son's disappearance could have turned out—at the bottom of a river or, lured by a cute puppy, in the trunk of a predator's car.

Jamil's death pointed out what every parent knows but tries not to fixate on—that no matter how vigilant you try to be, you cannot watch them every second of every day, especially as they grow into teens. As much as you try to teach them to act responsibly, you cannot control their actions.

### Ascribing Blame

And yet something the boy's family said after his death bothered me. Family members were upset that the boys were able to make their way down the steep embankment to the water.

"If there had been a fence up there, they wouldn't have gone that route," Jamil's aunt, Janet Guy, told reporters.

A grieving aunt can be forgiven for seeking a scapegoat on whom to blame this tragedy.

For dreaming there is someone out there—government, society, somebody—capable of wailing our children away from danger.

But it would have to be a mighty wall and an endless one, too, long enough and high enough and impenetrable enough to protect every child from every conceivable hazard.

From every creek and pond and railroad track and cliff and lurking stranger.

If only there had been a fence . . .

If only it were that simple.

It is easy for parents whose children are safe today to pass judgment. To say Jamil and his cousins should have been more closely supervised; should have been better trained to avoid danger. I won't be among them.

I've had my brush with the fenceless world and know this: Jamil could have been Conor and Conor Jamil. One boy's tragedy, another's close call.

In life, there are no foolproof fences, no impervious cocoons. Only little children and the adults who do their best to keep them safe.

*⌐⌐⌐⌐⌐⌐⌐ August 29, 2005*

## "It's Never the Same"
### *Too True*

I was running late.

At the end of the long hallway, the last room on the right sat empty.

The bed was made, a walker in the corner. My mother and her wheelchair were missing.

I found a nurse. "I'm Ruth Grogan's son. Is my mother around?"

It was a dumb question. This was a nursing home. Of course she was around. Everyone was always around.

"I'd try the chapel," the nurse offered. "Mass started at 11."

Life has its chapters, distinct divisions marked by watershed events, and this summer marked a new one in mine. A year earlier, when I had visited my aging parents at their home outside Detroit, ripe tomatoes lined the windowsill, a pot of soup simmered on the stove, and my folks greeted me happily at the door.

This summer's visit marked a new beginning. As my children swam in the lake I had swum in as a boy, I sifted through my father's papers, visited his grave, and spent time with my mother in the place she now calls home.

As far as nursing homes go, it's a lovely one, perched on a shaded hill overlooking a lake and run by kind nuns committed to compassionate care. But it is still a nursing home with all the smells and sounds and sadness nursing homes hold.

I made my way down corridors lined with frail women passing the hours. "Take me with you," one of them pleaded as I passed.

### Bowed White Heads

In the chapel, an ancient priest celebrated Mass before a small clutch of nuns and about three dozen patients, their wheelchairs arranged in an arc around the altar. From behind, the bowed white heads all looked alike. As I scanned the congregates, I realized nearly all of them were asleep. My mother was no exception.

I touched her shoulder and whispered, "Hi, Ruthie." Her eyes opened and widened with surprise. She had forgotten I was coming.

My 89-year-old mother's memory has been fleeing her for some years now. When my father died in December, she lost not only her husband of 58 years but a devoted and exceptionally attentive 24/7 caregiver.

Mom's eyes shut again, and I stood with my hands on her shoulders as the priest soldiered on. At Communion, he walked down the rows of wheelchairs, placing wheat hosts onto tongues. My mother woke to accept hers and, as she always has, pressed a fist to her heart and began working her lips in silent prayer.

Some things are not easily lost.

After Mass, I wheeled her into the courtyard, where she tilted her head toward the sun and smiled. Deep lines crossed her face, and her hair was as snowy as a blizzard. But a child's face looked up at me, a little girl lost in her innocence.

### A Song from Long Ago

She began to hum and then sing. It was a song I had never heard before, a ditty about a brash child swallowed by an alligator she thought she could tame. Mom had no idea what she had eaten for breakfast that morning, but she reeled effortlessly through the stanzas, not missing a beat.

"Where did you learn that?" I asked.

"Girl Scouts," she said.

I had to laugh. "That was 80 years ago! It's about time you sang it to me." Then she sang it all over again.

We sat quietly for a moment. She broke the silence with an observation.

"Once they leave home, that's it," she volunteered as if she were telling it to someone other than one of those who had left. "They come back to visit, but it is never the same."

I wanted to insist otherwise, but she was right. It never is. It never was.

I wheeled her back to her room and kissed her goodbye.

"I'll be back this evening with Jenny and the kids," I told her. What I did not say is that the next morning we would be returning to Pennsylvania.

Outside in the parking lot, I looked back through her room window where I had left her. She was peering out at something far, far away. When I caught her attention, a startled look of pleasant surprise came across her face, the same look she had given me at chapel. It was as if she were seeing me for the first time.

"Aw, Mom," I whispered.

She blew me a kiss. I blew one back, then drove away.

*October 17, 2005*

## Who's a Father? A Guy Who's There

I noticed them immediately.

Standing in front of me in line at a fast-food restaurant near Souderton on a rain-streaked Tuesday, the father and his daughter were hard to miss.

To a stranger's eye at first glance, they did not appear as if they belonged together.

She was 6 or 7, a pretty, delicate girl with sand-colored hair that fell to her shoulders. She was dressed sharply in a blue-and-green plaid jumper, white shirt, white anklets, and black dress shoes.

He was about 35, dressed in old jeans, a sleeveless T-shirt, and a ball cap worn backward over a bandana tied around his head. Both forearms sported large tattoos, and his face, dominated by a long mustache and scraggly goatee, spoke of a hard life. He used bad grammar.

He looked as if he belonged on a big Harley-Davidson, not here in line with a schoolgirl.

I don't even know for a fact that he was her father, but the longer I watched them, the more convinced of it I became. They had that certain easy chemistry that can exist between dads and their little girls.

They stood quietly in line, not talking. He rested his muscled arms on the counter; she leaned into him. He ordered their food, adding, "and one of them frosty things" for the girl.

### A Comfortable Silence

They sat a few tables from me and ate mostly in silence, but it was a comfortable, easy silence. He reached over and unwrapped her cheeseburger. She swung her legs beneath her as she chewed.

I noted with approval that he held back her frozen dessert until she had finished her meal. Then he sprinkled the topping on it a little at a time as she ate so each bite would be special.

It might say something about my own prejudices and stereotypes that I took notice of this rough-hewn, working-class guy simply meeting the minimum standards we'd expect of any parent. If he were dressed in a khaki suit and penny loafers, would I have looked twice?

I hope so. The special one-on-one bond between fathers and their daughters is one of life's more under-reported joys. And one worthy of notice.

When my daughter was a preschooler, I sometimes took her out to breakfast before work, just the two of us. No Mom Rules. We ate with our fingers, shared drinks from the same straw, and burped with abandon. Moments worth remembering after others have faded into dusk.

What struck me about this father and daughter was how effortlessly they interacted. He was not one of those smothering "quality-time" types jabbering and treating his child like a miniature adult at a cocktail party.

But he was there for her, and she for him. It was something to watch.

## Little Life Lessons

After the man and girl were done eating, he walked her to the bathroom and stood outside the door until she came out. She held her hands up to his nose so he could smell the soap, proof she had washed them.

At the door to the parking lot, she pulled. "Push," he said.

She pushed, the door swung open, and she looked up at him as if he were the smartest man alive.

As they stepped outside, it occurred to me that parenting is not rocket science. You don't need a doctoral degree in child development to be decent at it.

Sometimes it is as simple as saying push instead of pull.

Fathers, I was reminded, come in many shapes and sizes and fit no one mold. The good ones have a few things in common, and at the top of the list is just being there. Present and accounted for. There for the big moments, but also there for burgers at Wendy's on a rainy afternoon.

They stood beneath the awning for a moment, surveying the puddle-filled parking lot. The girl looked down at her new shoes, and then the man did, too. Without a word, he leaned over and scooped her up in one strong, tattooed arm. She tossed her arms around his neck, peachy cheek to ornery bristle, and together they headed off into the dampness.

She was with her dad, high and dry and safe in his arms. Did life for a little girl in a plaid jumper get any better than this?

*August 21, 2006*

## Learn the Rhythm of Solitude
### *A Backpack Hike Shows*
### *Grace that Comes in Solitude*

In the summer of 1977, I nearly sent my poor mother into cardiac arrest when I announced my plans to hitchhike and backpack around New England by myself.

"Alone?" Mom asked. "Oh no, you aren't."

"Mom," I shot back in my best this-time-you're-not-winning voice. "I'm going."

She began to protest, but my father caught her eye. He didn't breathe a word, but his face said it all. I know he's your baby. I know you worry. But he's not a child anymore. You need to let go.

My father knew what dwells in a young man's heart. He knew that sometimes a guy has to find adventure to find himself.

I had just finished my sophomore year of college and had a few weeks until my summer job started. I had hitchhiked and backpacked with friends before. Who knows what I was trying to prove, but this time I needed to do it alone.

When my father was 20, he was supporting a widowed mother and two younger siblings as he worked his way through college. Not long after, he was on an aircraft carrier in the South Pacific. He didn't need a solo road trip to prove his chops. But he seemed to understand that I did.

"Well, OK, then," my mother finally said. "But you better call."

We made a deal. I would phone every other day, and Mom would keep her worrying to herself.

I set out with everything I needed on my back. My first night out, I was ready to raise the white flag and go limping home.

I had gotten dropped off at a trailhead of the Appalachian Trail in western Massachusetts. Evening was fast approaching, and I hiked in only a couple of miles before setting up camp. Rather than put up my tent, I decided to sleep under the stars. As blackness enveloped me, coyotes began yipping all around. I swore I could hear them moving through the brush.

Then the rain started. I pulled a tarp over me and figured that would keep me dry enough. What seemed like hours later, I bolted awake, rainwater rushing in from where it had pooled atop the tarp. I was soaked.

I reached for my watch and hoped daybreak was imminent. The illuminated hands read 11:20 p.m. It was going to be a very long night.

At the first gray of dawn, I rose, wrung as much water as I could from my sleeping bag, and began to walk. By lunch the sun was out, and I spread my wet clothes and bedding over shrubs to dry. Yet my spirits remained damp. The steep terrain left me winded and with aching muscles. Blisters popped out on my feet. As much as I didn't want to admit it, I was miserable.

But I soldiered on, hiking through most of Massachusetts and into Vermont. With each day, my strength and confidence grew. I fell into a routine, rising with the sun, hiking until it began to slant low in the sky, then stopping to swim, cook over a small open fire, and fall asleep to the nocturnal sounds of nature.

The rhythm of solitude, once so intimidating, began to feel comfortable. Aloneness, I was learning, does not have to equal loneliness.

And when I had walked as far as I cared to walk, I put out my thumb and began to hitch my way around New England, stopping in villages and college towns, eventually making it to Boston.

In all the encounters with strangers, I came across just one creep. An oddly silent man who picked me up and when we reached my turnoff offered to drive me 20 miles out of his way if I'd only pose for a few photos. When I balked, he assured me they would just be snapshots of me standing beside the car. Why not, I figured. I was so clueless, it never occurred to me why he might be so motivated to collect photos of young strangers.

But he was the exception.

There was the young hippie girl who picked me up in a Volkswagen microbus (yes, stereotypes come from somewhere) and shared a cooler of vegetable sandwiches and cold beer with me. There were the graduate students in Amherst who fed me a big spaghetti dinner and let me sleep on their living room floor. There was the cop who found me with my thumb out on a desolate stretch of road and pulled a U-turn to give me a lift to a more traveled intersection. And the small-town folks everywhere who offered me cold drinks as I passed by.

For all the bad things in this world, I was learning a fundamental truth that people are basically good and kind and generous. You couldn't be dumb about it, but if you took a chance on them, the vast majority would not betray your trust.

That summer I came to appreciate the beauty of solitude and the gift of companionship. I learned to revel in nature and trust my instincts. Most important, I came to believe in the overarching decency of the human race.

Not a bad haul for one young man's summer sojourn.

# Animals

## What's Good for the Goose? Us

I've been talking to the geese lately.

"You guys," I say. "What's your problem? Can't you do any better than this? Shouldn't you be basking on a nice golf course in Florida?"

They look up at me like I'm some kind of quack and say what they always say. Honk!

Canada geese. The big, fat, beautiful birds are everywhere, ubiquitous ornaments on the suburban landscape. I pass them as I walk into the mall, drive by the cemetery, take my kids to the playground, visit college campuses and corporate parks, and turn into my neighborhood.

A whole big flock of them has taken over the lawn outside the door of my office, where they chew the frozen grass, ignoring the stream of humans trudging by just feet away.

What I don't get is why here? Greater Philadelphia has its virtues, but as a wild and scenic refuge for water fowl, it's got to be near the bottom of the list. Especially in

March with the snow, the ice, the salt, and that frumpy bulky-sweater look.

I've been trying to talk some sense into them. But do they listen? You would think they were teenagers.

"Excuse me," I tell them. "If I could fly to New Orleans for free, do you think I'd be standing here in a slush pile eating frozen grass? Hello? You've got wings. Use them."

Honk!

### Flap Southward, Dummies

"Look, I'll make it easy for you. I'll point, and you fly. It's not that complicated. South is that way. Just keep going until you hit Disney World. Go on. Shoo!"

Honk!

"All right. If you're not going to fly south for winter like any self-respecting goose would do, at least hang out at Valley Forge or some other open space. I mean, is a grimy industrial zone along the Schuylkill really your idea of a good time?"

It's no use. They just keep chewing and pooping, chewing and pooping.

I turn for help to a water-fowl professional, none other than the appropriately named Donald Drake, a wildlife specialist and assistant professor of wildlife management at Rutgers University.

Professor Drake, first things first. Is that really your name?

Absolutely, he assures me.

So how come these dumb geese insist on hanging out in the Philly deep freeze when they can be catching rays on Hilton Head Island?

Drake does not duck the question.

What we see around the 'burbs are not migratory geese, he explains. We see their plumper couch-potato cousins, which are so happy here they've made this their year-round home.

"They most likely never migrated a day in their life," Drake says.

And if they appear fearless, it's because they are, he says. The suburbs are essentially a predator- and hunting-free zone for geese, and they've figured out that we suburbanites are harmless weenies. (Oh yeah? Let them try stepping in front of our SUVs as we head home from work!)

### Creating an Ideal Habitat

We spend tens of thousands of dollars on everything from border collies to firecrackers to shoo away the winged eating machines. But basically they don't give a flying quack.

Drake points out that we've given them everything a goose could possibly ask for. "As Americans, we have a fascination with well-manicured grass," Drake says. And *Branta canadensis* thanks us for it.

Not only are our suburban lawns and soccer fields tasty, but we keep them nice and short, just how geese like them so no enemies can sneak up on them. And then we dig backyard ponds and subdivision drainage lakes, which they like, too. And we chase off most of the bird's natural predators. Some of us even feed them bread.

We've pretty much given geese everything they could ask for except their own cable channel. And, remind me again, which species is supposed to have the superior intellect?

"Most of their life they spend grazing and just loafing around," Drake says. "People ask, 'Wouldn't it be great to have a dog's life?' But to have a Canada goose's life, I think, would be even better."

Right. And now if you'll excuse me, I need to get back out there and take their drink orders.

*April 4, 2003*

# A Feline Air Traveler
# Lost in Philadelphia

Felix is MIA.

Missing in action, not on a battlefield in the Iraqi desert, but somewhere in the cavernous bowels in Philadelphia International Airport.

Felix is a cat.

The black feline with the white patch on his chest disappeared March 4 during a plane change in Philadelphia while en route from Baltimore to London to join his owners. No one has seen a trace of him since.

U.S. Airways, which was transporting the cat, has put out food and water, conducted several sweeps, posted Felix's photograph, even hired a tracker with a beagle to try to sniff the cat out of hiding. All to no avail.

His owners, while acknowledging that a lost feline is not exactly headline news, want him back desperately. So desperately that they have traveled the Atlantic Ocean and back again in search of him.

The story begins in Baltimore with Rebecca Smith, a British nanny, and her American husband, Darrell, an events planner. Earlier this year, the couple decided to return to England to be near Rebecca's parents.

Rebecca and the couple's 3-year-old daughter flew to London in January. Darrell and Felix the cat were to follow later. Darrell made it; Felix, locked in a pet carrier bearing a large "Live Animal" sticker, did not.

U.S. Airways admits a mistake was made. Said spokeswoman Amy Kudwa: "We continue our very diligent efforts to find the animal, [which] at this time has not been found."

## The Wrong Conveyor Belt

A baggage handler was supposed to take Felix to a cargo area to receive food and water and await transfer. Instead, a cargo manager told the Smiths, the employee accidentally put Felix's carrier on a conveyor belt that took him on a journey into the airline's cavernous luggage area.

When workers finally located the carrier, the door was ajar, and Felix was gone. "I just find it absolutely amazing that in a space of about 20 minutes they lost an 18-pound cat," Rebecca Smith, 34, told me by telephone from England.

Three days after the disappearance, U.S. Airways flew the couple back to Philadelphia and put them up in a hotel overnight so they could comb the baggage area to lure their shy cat out of hiding. Felix, if he was still in the building, wasn't taking the bait.

"It was very much a wasted trip," Darrell Smith said. "We want our cat back; that's the main thing. But I don't think that's going to happen. It's been a month now."

While the airline insists the search continues, the Smiths sense otherwise.

"I don't think they're really worried about it anymore," Darrell Smith said.

The Smiths said the airline has agreed to refund Felix's $257 ticket and has told them to submit a bill for the price of the cat.

Said Rebecca Smith: "We got him from a shelter when he was two months old. Monetarily, the cat has no value."

## A Loyal Friend

But to the family, Felix is a priceless family member. The big lazy cat helped Rebecca through many homesick nights in America and became a constant companion to the couple's daughter, Dominique. "It was like he was guarding her," the wife said.

"If it were lost clothing, we wouldn't care. You can replace clothing," she said. Then, perhaps realizing how her concern for a cat might sound amid the mounting human casualties of war, she added: "You can't really understand unless you are a cat person."

Or at least a pet person. We know better, but still we treat them like children, spoiling them, worrying over them, grieving when they die.

Tellingly, the couple have begun to speak of their pet in the past tense, even as the relationship between the couple and U.S. Airways grows increasingly tense. The Smiths say airline officials are impatient with the family's continued insistence on finding Felix. As for her part, Kudwa, the airline's spokeswoman, won't discuss details of the case, citing fear of a lawsuit—a possibility the Smiths deny.

As hope for locating their pet of seven years fades, the couple has a request of the people of Philadelphia. If anyone spots a big black cat with a white tuft on his chest, please give a call.

There's a family across the ocean who very much wants him home again.

*January 6, 2004*

## Saying Farewell to a Faithful Pal

In the gray of dawn, I found the shovel in the garage and walked down the hill to where the lawn meets the woods. There, beneath a wild cherry tree, I began to dig.

The earth was loose and blessedly unfrozen, and the work went fast. It was odd being out in the backyard without Marley, the Labrador retriever who for 13 years made it his business to be tight by my side for every excursion out the door, whether to pick a tomato, pull a weed, or fetch the mail. And now here I was alone, digging him this hole.

"There will never be another dog like Marley," my father said when I told him the news that I finally had to put the old guy down. It was as close to a compliment as our pet ever received.

No one ever called him a great dog—or even a good dog. He was as wild as a banshee and as strong as a bull. He crashed joyously through life with gusto most often associated with natural disasters.

He's the only dog I've ever known to get expelled from obedience school.

Marley was a chewer of couches, a slasher of screens, a slinger of drool, a tipper of trash cans. He was so big he could eat off the kitchen table with all four paws planted on the floor—and did so whenever we weren't looking.

Marley shredded more mattresses and dug through more drywall than I care to remember, almost always out of sheer terror brought on by his mortal enemy, thunder.

### Cute but Dumb

Marley was a majestic animal, nearly 100 pounds of quivering muscle wrapped in a luxurious fur coat the color of straw. As for brains, let me just say he chased his tail till the day he died, apparently convinced he was on the verge of a major canine breakthrough.

That tail could clear a coffee table in one swipe. We lost track of things he swallowed, including my wife's gold necklace, which we eventually recovered, shinier than ever. We took him with us once to a chi-chi outdoor café and tied him to the heavy wrought-iron table. Big mistake. Marley spotted a cute poodle and off he bounded, table in tow.

But his heart was pure.

When I brought my wife home from the doctor after our first pregnancy ended in miscarriage, that wild beast gently rested his blocky head in her lap and whimpered. And when babies finally arrived, he somehow understood they were something special and let them climb all over him, tugging his ears and pulling out little fistfuls of fur. One day when a stranger tried to hold one of the children, our jolly giant showed a ferocity we never imagined was inside him.

As the years passed, Marley mellowed, and sleeping became his favorite pastime. By the end, his hearing was shot, his teeth were gone, his hips so riddled with arthritis he barely could stand. Despite the infirmities, he greeted each day with the mischievous glee that was his hallmark. Just days before his death, I caught him with his head stuck in the garbage pail.

### Life Lessons Learned

A person can learn a lot from a dog, even a loopy one like ours.

Marley taught me about living each day with unbridled exuberance and joy, about seizing the moment and following your heart. He taught me to appreciate the simple things—a walk in the woods, a fresh snowfall, a nap in a shaft of winter sunlight. And as he grew old and achy, he taught me about optimism in the face of adversity.

Mostly, he taught me about friendship and selflessness and, above all else, unwavering loyalty.

When his time came last week, I knelt beside him on the floor of the animal hospital, rubbing his gray snout as the veterinarian discussed cremation with me. No, I told her, I would be taking him home with me.

The next morning, our family would stand over the hole I had dug and say goodbye. The kids would tuck drawings in beside him. My wife would speak for us all when she'd say: "God, I'm going to miss that big, dumb lug."

But now I had a few minutes with him before the doctor returned. I thought back over his 13 years—the destroyed furniture and goofy antics, the sloppy kisses and utter devotion. All in all, not a bad run.

I didn't want him to leave this world believing all his bad press. I rested my forehead against his and said: "Marley, you are a great dog."

*January 13, 2004*

## They're Bad, and We Love 'Em Still

Man, and I thought my dog was bad.

Ever since I penned a farewell to my companion of 13 years, Marley the neurotic and incorrigible Labrador retriever, my e-mail inbox has resembled a TV talk show episode: "Bad Dogs—and the Humans Who Love Them!"

In the week since I wrote about Marley's death, I have heard from several hundred pet owners. They offered condolences (thanks, everyone). But mostly they wanted to dispute the accuracy of my report.

Now I know I erred when I characterized Marley as the planet's worst-behaved creature. The typical response went something like, "Your dog could not have been the worst because MY dog is the worst." And to prove the point, they supplied detailed accounts of shredded couches, raided cupboards, and sneak slobber attacks.

Oddly enough, nearly all the tales involved large retrievers, just like Marley.

Take it away, Sandy Chanoff of Abington Township: "Alex was what we called a 'high spirited Lab' with a little attention deficit disorder. He ate almost all of my leather shoes, pocketbooks, and even the carpet. He would greet us at the door with something in his mouth all the time, and would jump all around like he hadn't seen us in years. He knocked everything off the coffee table with his tail. By the way, we were also thrown out of obedience school." You too, huh?

### Diploma Envy

Gracie, a golden retriever owned by Lynne Major and Lynn Lampman of Drexel Hill, actually managed to graduate—and was so excited she promptly jumped up and pulverized her diploma. Said Major: "She is lovable and a little crazy at the same time."

Lois Finegan of Upper Darby said my manic mutt had nothing on her separation-anxiety-challenged Lab, Gypsy. "She was a holy terror in her day, eating curtains and their rods, doors, rugs, plants, and even a jalousie window."

Others reported their dogs gobbling down beach towels, sponges, kitty litter, spare change, even a diamond ring (which definitely trumps Marley's taste for gold necklaces).

Mike Casey of Pottstown beat them all. He said his late dog, Jason, a retriever-Irish setter mix, once downed a five-foot vacuum cleaner hose, coiled reinforcing wire and all—without so much as a burp.

Elyssa Burke of West Goshen feared the worst after her dog, Mo (yes, another highly intelligent Lab!), decided to exit the house by crashing through a second-story window. Mo survived the fall just fine, apparently quite delighted by his newly forged egress. "He landed on a shrub, which broke his fall," Burke explained.

Nancy Williams clipped my column on Marley because it reminded her of her own irrepressible retriever, Gracie. She writes: "I left the article on the kitchen table and turned to put away the scissors. When I turned back, sure enough, Gracie had eaten the column."

I'll take that as a compliment.

## Knee-Deep in Concrete

Rene Wick of Havertown owns "a lunk-headed yellow Lab named Clancy," who decided to make a lasting impression on the next-door neighbors by visiting their newly poured foundation. "Clancy jumped the fence and went straight into the still-wet concrete up to his knees," Wick wrote.

And then came Haydon, the brawny—not to be confused with brainy—Lab that once swallowed a tube of Super Glue. "His finest hour, however," owner Carolyn Etherington of Jamison recounted, "was when he tore the frame out of the garage door after I had foolishly attached his leash to it." She adds, "In those days, we had the veterinarian on speed dial."

Tim Manning of Yardley thought he had outfoxed his yellow Lab, Ralph, by stowing a chocolate centerpiece safely on top of the refrigerator. "Ralph figured out how to open a drawer on the linen cabinet next to the refrigerator and use it as a ladder," Manning wrote. "We could tell because the drawer's contents were all over the floor, and the chocolate was devoured right there on top of the fridge."

All of which raises the question that any sane person must be asking: If pets are this much of a pain, why does anyone keep them?

As Sharon Durivage of Yardley put it: "They give their love and loyalty freely and always forgive us for our bad days and cranky moods."

*September 21, 2004*

## Shelter in Media
## Mocks Its Mission

Who said it's a dog's life?

For the dogs—and cats—at the Delaware County SPCA, life is anything but.

As *The Inquirer*'s Barbara Boyer has illustrated in a series of articles, the private, nonprofit animal shelter in Media makes a mockery of its name—the Society for the Prevention of Cruelty to Animals.

Does an organization dedicated to animals prevent cruelty by cramming dogs and cats into crowded, unsanitary conditions?

By allowing contagious diseases to run rampant through the facility? By blithely adopting desperately sick animals out to unsuspecting families who then face either mountainous veterinarian bills or the heartbreak of putting down the animal—or both?

Does it prevent cruelty by sitting on a $7.6 million nest egg while refusing to provide a modicum of veterinary care for its animals? By having a veterinarian on premises just two hours a week? Two hours for a facility that last year handled nearly 3,000 dogs?

If this is where cruelty is prevented, I'd hate to see the torture chamber.

We humans expect certain minimum standards for our four-legged companions: safe, sanitary conditions, proper nutrition, clean drinking water, compassionate care, adequate medical attention.

It's not rocket science, and yet the shelter's 13-member board appears clueless on so many fronts, incapable of getting even the basics right.

## Goodwill Gone Bad

The negligence is not malicious. It's benign in nature, good intentions overwhelmed by poor decisions—or no decisions at all.

Part of the problem seems to be the board's inability to wisely tap its $7.6 million endowment. Even conservatively invested with a 4 percent return, the investment would yield more than $300,000 a year in income; at a 6 percent return, the shelter has $456,000 a year to play with. Yet the board members act like misers.

Nearly $8 million in the bank, and they can't afford $80,000 a year for a full-time veterinarian? Sorry, but that dog won't hunt.

"The board of directors just sits on the money," dog-rescue volunteer Arthur Herring the third of Mont-gomeryville told Boyer in frustration. "It's like a power trip for them."

Meanwhile, sick animals continue to go out to homes. Healthy animals continue to get infected. And the pathetic cycle continues.

Boyer has heard from people who adopted dogs and cats from the Delaware County shelter only to discover they were desperately ill. One woman took home a cat dying from the highly contagious feline HIV. Another adopted a German shepherd that spread a respiratory infection to the family's other dog. Yet another took home a pit bull mix, not knowing it was suffering from a highly contagious virus and internal bleeding. The dog required surgery, which cost the new owner $2,200.

### Redefining "Humane"

A Collingdale woman took home a dog suffering from kennel cough, worms, and malnourishment. "I could count every rib on her body," the owner told Boyer.

That's what one might expect from a back-alley puppy mill, not from a well-meaning group with the words "prevention of cruelty" in its title.

Volunteers have quit in disgust. Visiting veterinarians have complained about the conditions. The state vows to investigate. And yet the board digs in its heels, stubbornly defending its incompetence and clinging to its miserable Typhoid Mary methods.

When one former SPCA board member, Joseph P. Boyle, pushed to improve conditions at the shelter, he was forced off the board. Boyle told *The Inquirer* that sick but treatable dogs were often euthanized because death was cheaper than medicine.

What is going on here?

Some animal advocates have begun a petition drive to recall all 13 members of the shelter's board, and that is a good thing. Perhaps a complete change in leadership is what is needed to get this sorry excuse for an animal shelter back on track.

In the meantime, the existing board members need to tape reminders to their foreheads that read: "It's about preventing cruelty, stupid."

*June 6, 2005*

## Animal Lovers? No, Just Bullies

The far upper reaches of Bucks County still hold the vestiges of an earlier, simpler time.

Cows graze in pastures; tractors rumble along country lanes; open farmland, thousands of acres of it, stretches to the horizon, a quilt-work of browns and greens and golds.

It is a place where silos still outnumber cell-phone towers, and where stone farmhouses are actually still occupied by farmers with John Deeres, not investment bankers with BMWs.

A most unlikely scene for a brazen terrorist attack.

But it was here amid the pastoral tranquility of rural life in Richland Township, where the terrorists struck.

Not al-Qaeda or suicide bombers, but animal-rights activists.

Their cause: to keep animals from being used for medical research.

The innocent victims of their carnage: plants. Specifically, Chinese peonies, many of them rare and expensive, all of them ethereally beautiful.

I pull my car off Route 212 into the flower farm known as Peony Land, and the first thing I notice are the endless rows of blooming shrubs. Their fragrance fills the air; their vivid colors dab the fields like oil paints from an artist's palette.

## A Rich Irony

The next thing I notice are the obscenities scrawled in spray paint across the farm's barn. "[Very bad word] with primates, and get [very bad word] by us," it states.

The vandals used the acronym ALF—Animal Liberation Front.

The intended recipients are Peony Land owner Michael Hsu and his parents, Chao and Susan Hsu, who had planned to build a kennel on the 47-acre property to house up to 500 monkeys for medical research.

The vandals poured paint stripper on two cars and spray-painted several buildings on the property. But what broke the Hsus' hearts were the plants. The vandals dumped and smashed hundreds of delicate, high-end tree peonies in a greenhouse.

"I was in disbelief that people would do such a thing," Michael Hsu told me. "To spray-paint our buildings and write graffiti is one thing, but . . . these are plants. They have nothing to do with our application."

I'm sure the culprits who trashed Peony Land didn't intend it, but they left behind rich irony—the wanton and indiscriminate destruction of one living species to save another. Kill a plant, save a primate. Fauna ranks; flora apparently does not.

In someone's twisted mind, it all makes perfect sense.

Another irony: The primates the Hsus had planned to import would play a role in research that could someday cure deadly scourges such as AIDS and cancer. They could help in fight against bio-terror. Or as Hsu put it, they could help "to extend the lives and save the lives of millions of people."

## Thuggish Tactics

For the extremists masquerading as animal lovers, that is not enough, even if the monkeys are treated humanely, as Hsu insists they would be.

In an anonymous Web posting, a group claiming responsibility for the vandalism at Peony Land used the favorite method of thugs, terrorists, and bullies everywhere—intimidation.

"Drop your plans for a primate prison, or we will make your life a living hell," the posting states. "If you continue to go forward with your plans, we will destroy your business, and we will destroy your lives."

In what Hsu insists is an unfortunate coincidence, the family has withdrawn its application to house monkeys on its farm. Their decision, Hsu said, has nothing to do with the threats, but simply because he realized his proposal would not meet township space requirements.

That may be so, but he and I both know that the criminals who targeted him are crowing victory right now.

Reasonable people can disagree on the use of animals in medical experiments. But there are legitimate forums for airing such differences. A free society gives us that gift.

There is a word for those who instead would sneak around under cover of darkness and use anonymous postings to seed fear and intimidation: cowards. And with the Hsu family's sudden reversal, my fear is the cowards will only be emboldened.

*November 22, 2005*

## In the Next Ring, a Stepford Terrier

I spent Sunday immersed in a world that has gone totally, unapologetically to the dogs.

Believe me when I tell you fur was flying everywhere.

Not only was it flying, it was being combed, parted, clipped, teased, blow-dried, poofed, and puffed. The last time I witnessed this much vanity preening, I was walking past a beauty salon on the Main Line.

The occasion was the Kennel Club of Philadelphia Dog Shows, which stretched across two days and 15 rings in the Fort Washington Expo Center over the weekend, drawing 2,700 purebred dogs of every imaginable shape and size, accompanied by their perfection-driven owners, who also came in every imaginable shape and size.

Some 15,000 dog lovers streamed through the doors to ooh and ahh over the super pooches, and it occurred to me that if the Miss America contest could capture a fraction of this mojo, it wouldn't be going down the drain.

In the staging area, the owners fretted over their pooches, which waited patiently for their turn before the judges. Many of these dogs live a good part of their lives on the road, going from one show to the next. I watched as a spectator patted a husky on the head, and his handler swooped with a comb to fluff the violated spot.

### Racing to Nowhere

I knew I was in a special world all its own when I headed for the bathroom and found not only His and Her doors, but Human and Canine facilities, too. The dogs actually got the better deal, enjoying spotless stalls filled with sweet-smelling cedar shavings.

In the rings, the handlers lined up their unflinchingly behaved specimens and began prancing around in circles at a half-run under the keen eyes of the judges. Round and round they trotted, hurrying to go nowhere.

A surprising number of the handlers were young people, many in their early teens. They obviously had invested hundreds if not thousands of hours into working with their dogs. What was up with these kids? Shouldn't they have been home playing video games?

The dogs were something to behold. They stood in flawless formation, their noses just inches from the tails of the dogs in front of them. Not one of them made a move. No lunges, no butt-sniffing, no hopping in the air as if they had invisible springs on their paws. No attempts at intimate relations. No two-legged floor dances. It was like I was watching fur-clad robots that had been programmed by Miss Manners.

Who was the official sponsor of this show, anyway? Puppy Prozac?

As the unofficial chairman and spiritual leader of the Dysfunctional Dog Owners of America, I'll admit to a little professional jealousy. I couldn't help imagining how my own late and not-so-great Labrador retriever, Marley, would have taken the competition by storm, starting by stealing the tablecloth off the judges' table.

If the kennel club had a shredded-couch division, I'd have had a shoo-in national champion.

### Optional Commands

The current Lab-in-residence at the Grogan house thinks "Come!" is a suggestion she is happy to take under advisement and get back to us on. She's never met a rustling leaf that hasn't been worth barking herself hoarse over.

Every dog has its strengths, and Gracie's unique gift is her eye-tongue coordination. This allows her to leap into the air and smash her snout into our faces at the exact moment we are opening our mouths to speak, allowing her to jam her tongue where no canine tongue was meant to go. We call her the Phantom Frencher.

And she's the good one.

I guess I came to the show hoping to find some small ray of hope that even award-winning show dogs shared some common ground with my obedience-school rejects.

I scrutinized the contestants for any cracks in their glossy armor. C'mon, I pleaded silently, just one flying drool-stringer. Nothing. They trotted; they pranced; they posed, not missing a beat. I came across one poodle, so still and perfectly coifed, I had to look twice to confirm it wasn't stuffed.

"That's just not right," I said.

As much as I envied the magnificent über-beasts, I knew that life for them, as for all of us, was full of trade-offs.

Good dogs win all the ribbons, it's true. But bad dogs have more fun.

*⌒ January 31, 2006*

## Marley & Me
### *The Whole Truth*

In light of the scandal enveloping best-selling author James Frey, who now admits his purportedly nonfiction memoir *A Million Little Pieces* is riddled with fabrications and exaggerations, the online accuracy watchdog

SmokingCanine.com has launched an investigation into another memoir currently topping best-seller lists. We now bring you this shocking expose:

PHILADELPHIA—Credible evidence has surfaced that *Inquirer* columnist John Grogan might have greatly exaggerated the badness of his now-infamous Labrador retriever Marley.

In his memoir, *Marley & Me: Life and Love with the World's Worst Dog*, Grogan portrays his now-deceased pet as incorrigible, neurotic, ill-mannered, flatulent and slobbering. But a SmokingCanine investigation found scant evidence to support the unflattering depiction.

One former neighbor, Betty Barcalot, told Smoking-Canine: "Marley was a great dog. I once witnessed him dart into traffic to pull a Chihuahua to safety. But did that make the book?"

Added a former nanny: "Yes, there was a lot of damage to the house, but you should ask Mr. Grogan about how it got there. Let me just say an incompetent homeowner with power tools can be a dangerous thing."

### Ice Picks and Drool

Reports that Grogan may have used an ice pick to intentionally mar his home's woodwork in an attempt to frame Marley could not be confirmed.

Even Grogan's wife, Jenny, has distanced herself from the book, saying, "Honestly, if anyone had a drooling problem, it was my husband."

Grogan now admits the amount of saliva produced by the hound was exaggerated. "I swear, it seemed like gallons at the time," he said in a brief interview.

Grogan's book claimed Marley "chased his tail till the day he died." But family veterinarian Andover Yorecash called the claim, "absurd . . . beyond laughable." He added: "On the numerous occasions Marley was in to have a household object extracted from his bowels, I never once saw him chase his tail."

At a dog park Marley was known to frequent, a Rottweiler who gave his name only as "Fritz" said the whole book is a gross exaggeration.

Speaking through an interpreter, he growled, "Never once did I see Marley sniff a poodle's butt. And even if he did, is that so wrong?"

Fritz added: "I knew Marley. Marley was a friend of mine. The character in this book is no Marley."

Dutchess, a corgi who was once romantically linked to the buff Labrador, added: "Grogan makes a big deal out of Marley's nutty behavior, but he was nothing special. Hello! He's a male Lab. They all act like that."

SmokingCanine has learned that literally hundreds of Labrador retriever owners have come forward to dispute Grogan's "world's worst dog" contention.

## Window Jumpers

Said one, "I know with certainty that Marley wasn't the worst. Did he ever jump out of a second-story window like my Bunky?"

Grogan admitted Marley only crashed through first-floor windows.

There are even as-yet-unsubstantiated rumors that Marley is not dead at all but living in seclusion in a canine rest home in Boca Raton, Florida.

"I can't swear it's the same dog," said Rocco De-Rawhyde, an aide at the facility. "But our resident, 'Harley,' is a dead ringer for that dog on the cover. All I know is just before the book comes out, these two guys in sunglasses drop him off with strict orders, 'No visitors, no media interviews.'"

Attempts to locate "Harley" were unsuccessful.

Grogan refused to comment about allegations that his original title for the book was *My Marley, My Dream Dog*, and that he only changed the premise after his agent could not sell the manuscript, saying, "The whole Lassie thing is SO last year."

Oprah Winfrey, who recently withdrew her endorsement of *A Million Little Pieces*, did not return calls seeking comment on this latest controversy.

*February 27, 2006*

## Zoo Hysteria High as Elephant's Eye

It might be easy to write off as a nutty extremist Marianne Bessey, the animal-rights activist who has been banned from the Philadelphia Zoo.

Easy, that is, until you look into the eyes of the giant, majestic beasts she so zealously—some might say hysterically—champions.

Until you look into the eyes of a captive elephant.

There is something there. Something more than docile existence. There is intelligence, fierce intelligence. No question about it. Even the zoo's own Web site notes the animal's innate smarts. Is it my imagination, or is there also sadness in those eyes?

### Sadness and Longing?

Bessey thinks there is, and she has become obsessed with helping the zoo's four elephants find freedom—or at least a relative facsimile of it—at a 2,700-acre pachyderm sanctuary in Tennessee.

She has become a major burr under the saddle of the zoo's administration, regularly visiting the elephants in their tight quarters at the zoo, videotaping them, freely sharing her opinion that elephants deserve better than a quarter-acre exercise yard where visitors stand and gawk at them.

"They're so intelligent and just so amazing," she said by phone Friday.

### "A Little Depressed"

Bessey, a lawyer, became smitten with elephants as a child. "But when I saw them in circuses or zoos, I always felt there's something wrong here," she said. "They always seemed a little off or depressed."

In 1996, she traveled to Zimbabwe to watch wild elephants in their native habitat and was stunned by how differently they behaved and interacted from confined animals.

And those smart, deep eyes, she insists, had different expressions. Not sad at all.

She calls zoo elephants mere "shadows" of wild elephants.

Last year she began badgering zoo officials to release the four elephants to the sanctuary where they could live closer to how nature intended. So far, the idea has gone nowhere.

She's particularly frustrated over the fate of Dulary, a 42-year-old female with an injury that has kept her inside a concrete barn since August.

"It's like putting your child in a closet for the rest of their life," she said.

As her frustration grew, she posted a message earlier this month on an online chat room known as the Elephant Connection. In it, she wished that Philadelphia Zoo Director Alexander L. "Pete" Hoskins might experience what it would be like to be "kept in a concrete closet for six months to hasten [his] demise."

"My frustration just boiled over," she said.

What she didn't know was that zoo officials were monitoring the chat room (your donor dollars at work), and they filed a police complaint against her, apparently on the theory that her comments were not-quite-but-almost-sort-of a little like a death threat.

### A Threat, but to What?

Now, we can't have death-threatening eco-terrorists at a family attraction, right? And so the activist was banned from zoo property.

Remind me again who's acting with extreme hysteria?

Let's get real here. The threat the zoo is trying to contain is not to its director's life but to its well-coifed public-relations image. Zoos are friendly, family places where all the animals are happy all the time. There is no room for loudmouths questioning whether the elephants might be better off running free.

I like zoos. I like the Philadelphia Zoo in particular, so much so that I have an annual membership. I like taking my kids there. But I have to say, when I reach the elephant enclosure, I see it, too. Those eyes.

Most of the animals seem content in their enclosures. But the elephants always leave me feeling just a little . . . sad. If they could talk, you know what they would say. And it would not be how splendid life is standing in a rectangle of dust so people can take their photographs.

Other major zoos have released their pachyderms to large sanctuaries where they now roam free.

Visit the zoo, look into those deep, knowing eyes. Then ask yourself: Isn't it time Philadelphia did the same?

*July 7, 2006*

## Puppy Mills Not Always Obvious

The sign rose out of the cornfields as we drove down a narrow country lane in far rural Berks County:

"Vegetables & puppies for sale."

This was the place. The place we had been looking for. Our longtime Labrador retriever, Marley, had died a few months earlier, and the silence in our home had become deafening.

It was time for another dog.

We were responding to a small classified ad for puppies of mixed but distinct lineage—a cross between two types of retrievers. After our wildly hyperactive purebred Lab, the mix sounded like a good bet. The breeders were old-time, traditional farmers who raised dogs on the side.

I pulled up to the old stone farmhouse where Jenny, our three children, and I were greeted by six stunningly beautiful youngsters. They were blond and blue-eyed, their skin burnished from working in the fields. The girls wore bonnets and calico dresses to their ankles. The boys wore overalls and brimmed hats. All were barefoot. No adults were in sight.

Jenny and I exchanged a smile. We both felt good about this place. A small family farm out of yesteryear; the real thing. We liked the idea of steering clear of commercial breeders, some of whom have reputations for being motivated more by profit than love of animals.

## A Sinking Feeling

I asked to see the puppies, and the oldest of the siblings, a girl about 16, stepped forward and without a word led us toward a cacophony of barking. Near the barn we found a series of rickety runs filled with dogs of every imaginable shape, size, and age. None looked like the progeny of two pure-bred dogs.

Two of the cages were rigged with spinning wire treadmills, like giant versions of the exercise wheels found in hamster cages, in which little yapping dogs raced endlessly. At once the scene was comical and heartbreaking.

It instantly felt wrong.

We began absorbing more of the scene. The puppies were crowded into a makeshift pen, and some looked lethargic with runny eyes and noses. Excrement covered the ground so thick it was almost impossible not to step in. The mother dogs slinked around the periphery of the barnyard, looking worn out and exhausted, their teats hanging low.

It was becoming obvious this was not the idyllic rural breeder we had imagined, and that these dogs were being bred and sold irresponsibly by children without visible adult supervision. We asked if the parents were available, but got no clear answer.

Still, we persevered. Anyone who has ever taken young children to pick out a puppy knows how difficult it is to leave empty-handed. The puppies, even the sickly ones, were undeniably cute, and the farm kids handed them out of the cage one at a time for my children to cuddle.

"This one, Dad; can we get this one?" they shouted for each puppy.

### Nervous Glances

Jenny and I exchanged nervous glances. We both knew we would not be leaving with one of these dogs.

I called the kids over to the car for a huddle. "We're going to get a puppy very soon," I promised. "But this is not the right place." The kids hung their heads but didn't protest. I think even they knew something was amiss.

As darkness fell over the unlit farm, we excused ourselves and drove away. A mile down the road, I pulled over and we all scraped dog dirt off our shoes.

It didn't occur to me that night, or for months after-
ward, that what we had stumbled on was a puppy mill.
Not one of the factorylike commercial enterprises Pennsylvania is so notorious for, but a puppy mill nonetheless.
A place that cranks out living animals like widgets for
profit and often passes along hereditary and health problems. Governor Rendell is taking steps to crack down on
these operations, and I applaud him for it.

Looking back on my experience two years later, I regret not doing more myself. I should have made a phone
call, should have turned them in. But these beautiful,
simple children were not what I imagined or wanted to
believe puppy-mill operators could be.

A puppy mill, I now know, can take many forms. Sometimes you don't even recognize it until it is too late.

*July 16, 2006*

## Celebrity & Me

Look what Marley has dragged in now. Best-sellerdom is
an unexpected and rich blessing, but at times the author
has a bone to pick.

I know exactly when and where it happened—the moment I finally figured out that my quiet, contented, boring little life had changed in powerful ways and would
not be changing back again anytime soon.

It was 8:30 a.m. on January 13, and I was sitting in the greenroom at the CBS studios in New York, waiting to go on *The Early Show*. A makeup artist powdered my nose and fussed with my hair. A producer wired me with a microphone.

I was there to talk about my book, *Marley & Me*, and its surprising vault from obscurity to the top of national best-seller lists.

Waiting in the wings with me to appear in the same half hour of the morning talk show were rapper/actress Queen Latifah, movie mogul Jerry Bruckheimer, and two young women with hardly any clothes on who billed themselves as "the world's only twin belly dancers."

"Only on morning television," host Harry Smith cracked to me moments before we went on the air. I just shook my head. The scene was surreal, and I was smack in the middle of it, about to go live in front of 2.7 million viewers.

After my interview, Smith leaned in close to me and, in an almost fatherly way, said, "I don't think you fully realize it yet, but your life will never be the same."

He knew what I was just beginning to understand. For better or worse, my new status as "best-selling author" would change everything, even as I resisted change with every fiber of my being.

I felt a little like the ordinary working schmo who wins the lottery. No, scratch that. I was the ordinary working schmo who won the lottery—my case, the lottery being the infinitesimally tiny chance of writing a first book that, for whatever mysterious combination of factors, takes off.

What began in my mind as a "little book"—the simple story of the early years of my marriage and the joyously insane Labrador retriever that would change the family we became—is now in its thirtieth printing, with just less than two million copies in print. It has been on the *New York Times* nonfiction hardcover best-seller list for 34 straight weeks, 16 of them at No. 1.

Part of me is ecstatic at this startling success. Part of me still can't quite believe it. And part of me worries about what effect it will have on my family, particularly my three children, and on my lifestyle, my career, my friendships.

I catch myself wondering: How did I get on this roller coaster, and how do I hold on?

The journey began on January 6, 2003, when I published a column in *The Inquirer* saying goodbye to my hopelessly hyperactive, incorrigible Labrador retriever Marley, who for 13 years filled our home and lives with riotous bedlam. He was a very bad boy yet with a heart as boundless as a summer sky, and I wanted to set the record straight after years of making fun of his total lack of self-control.

That column brought a flood of responses from *Inquirer* readers, responses that were highly personal. It was then I knew I had quite accidentally tapped into something bigger, something seminal. Not a dog story. Not my story. But the story of the journey humans and animals make together, and how the two shape and affect each other and become magically intertwined.

After a dozen rejections, I found an agent, Laurie Abkemeier, who saw the potential in my story and decided to take a chance on me. I began rising at 4:30 a.m.

to write before leaving for work. Week by week, chapter by chapter, the story spilled out like utterances from a hypnotized patient, without hand-wringing or self-consciousness.

Very early in the process I realized I could not tell the tale of this bigger-than-life dog without telling the tale of my wife, Jenny, and me and the life we were just beginning. The two stories were inseparable, one and the same.

The book flowed easily out of me partially because I was convinced no one would ever see it. As the book progressed, my agent kept telling me I was on to something, but I didn't quite believe her. I kept wondering: Who in their right mind would want to read 300 pages about my ho-hum life?

But when the manuscript was done, in fall 2004, the agent's instinct proved more accurate than the author's. She called me back a few days after shopping it around to say she had six publishers interested in making offers. We sold *Marley & Me* to the William Morrow Co., and it hit bookstores in mid-October 2005, debuting at No. 10 on the *Times* list.

My publisher's aggressive marketing and publicity campaign—it gave away thousands of early copies to reviewers, media types, and booksellers—gave me the big push it needed out of the gate.

But by the holidays, I became aware that something else was at play. *Marley's* rise above the glut of holiday-released books was being fueled in large part by that elusive gift—word-of-mouth buzz. Bookstore owners were recommending my book to their customers, librarians to their patrons and, most important, readers to their friends and relatives.

Attendance at my book signings was growing exponentially, from 40 or 50 in the early weeks to as many as 400.

And people were beginning to show up with multiple copies of my book in their arms. At one appearance in Chester County just before Christmas, I signed a copy for a woman who tracked me down the next week to sign 25 more copies she had decided to give as gifts.

By the time I appeared on *The Early Show*, *Marley & Me* was No. 3 on the *Times* list. A few weeks later, I was sitting in *The Inquirer's* downtown newsroom when Mauro DiPreta, my editor at William Morrow, called, as he did every Wednesday evening when the best-seller list was updated.

But this call was different; he was on a speaker phone surrounded by my entire publishing team. "Are you sitting down?" he asked. "Because you just hit No. 1."

All I could say was, "Wow."

I was similarly speechless in late January when I learned —by cell phone as I attended an author's reception with my wife in South Florida—that Fox 2000 Pictures had bought the film rights. I put my hand over the phone and whispered, "You won't believe this; they want to make a movie about us."

Jenny, who had graciously agreed to let me trot out the most personal details of her life in the book, just smiled nervously.

The routine of our life was changing dramatically. I was writing my *Inquirer* column and fielding a growing list of

media and public-appearance requests. And I was beginning my next book-writing projects.

The irony of my success was not lost on me—or my
family. I had written a book celebrating the simple joys of
life—and now there was precious little room for those joys.

In early March, I took a leave from *The Inquirer* to go
back on the road promoting the book—Chicago, Seattle,
Portland, San Francisco, Los Angeles, Jacksonville, New
York, Washington. Jenny felt like a single parent; on phone
calls home, I got the impression my kids were figuring out
how to get on without me around.

And when I was at home, a steady parade of media
people arrived at our door for interviews and photographs. Most of them made me proud of my profession.
They were smart, talented, fair-minded, and gracious. A
few reminded me why reporters are not always liked or
trusted.

In February, I was in Phoenix when I began receiving
e-mails saying, "Do you know Howard Stern's talking
about you on his show?"

Oh no, I thought, this can't be good. Stern, with his
bombastic and bawdy antics, was the last person I would
expect to click with my book.

But there he was on his satellite radio program for three
straight days telling the story of reading the conclusion of
*Marley & Me* while on a cross-country flight and weeping
so openly a flight attendant asked if he needed help.

He told his listeners he planned to write me a letter
telling me what the book meant to him. I thought he was
just blowing smoke, but a week later, a four-page handwrit-
ten letter arrived from Stern, and it was—lovely. Sensitive

and warm. I now know what I long suspected, that there is more to people than they sometimes let on, and there can be more to the jock than just shock.

My favorite part of this white-knuckle ride has been the people I've met along the way. Some have been celebrities, such as Diane Sawyer, who interviewed me on ABC's *Good Morning America*, and Anderson Cooper, who I met at a publishing party a week before his book knocked mine out of the No. 1 slot. Most have been ordinary readers, from as close as Ardmore and as far away as Australia, many of whom now seem like dear family friends.

They have formed a sort of Marley fraternity, sharing their photographs and stories at marleyandme.com and making friends with one another as they wait in line at signings. Some write me poems, some record goofy songs, some bake gourmet dog treats for our new Lab, Gracie. In Denver, 180 strangers sang "Happy Birthday" to me.

An amateur artist shipped me a beautiful framed portrait of Marley she painted in oils, which I hung in my bedroom.

Each morning, I look at his likeness staring out at me and just smile at the bizarre thought that my slobbering, never-do-right hound has become a household name, not just in the United States but, with Marley now being published in 24 languages, around the world.

When I was on leave from *The Inquirer*, many readers wrote to ask me if I was gone for good. I have to admit, I thought about it. But I love newspapers, this one in particular. I love writing a column and, above all else, I love the readers who follow and respond to my work.

After my first column back, a slew of messages greeted me, like this: "Yo, Grogan! Welcome back. Now get to work!"

Yep, there's no place like Philadelphia.

On the home front, best-sellerdom has been mostly an incomprehensible blessing but, as with most things in life, not without its trade-offs.

My sons, 14 and 12, are like most teenagers in that they crave anonymity. The book has thrust them out of that comfortable invisibility, and sometimes they struggle with the notoriety. Many of their classmates, and nearly all their teachers, have read the book. People stop them at school events or the mall to ask about it, making them squirm uncomfortably.

I can't protect them from that, but Jenny and I have decided to make no major lifestyle changes anytime soon. We plan to stay put. Our house is our home (although we might add that new kitchen we've long dreamed of), our neighbors, our friends, our local school system, our children's universe. Besides, I can't think of anyplace else I'd rather live.

I've always celebrated frugal simplicity. I am the guy who fixes broken appliances, washes my own car rather than fork over 10 bucks at the car wash, and scouts garage sales for steals. The income from the book and movie rights is something we had never dreamed of and something that will take some getting used to.

I upgraded my car, paid off some debts, bought Jenny the piano she had always wanted, and splurged on a nice family vacation to the Florida Keys. But mostly we want to invest for the future—and share some with those less fortunate.

Who could have imagined that dumb lughead dog of ours would put all three of our children through college and give us a secure retirement nest egg? Good dog, Marley!

As far as my children are concerned, all the hubbub can end anytime now.

One night recently as I tucked my 9-year-old daughter in bed after 10 days on the road, she looked up at me and said without a trace of self-pity: "You know what, Dad? I'm kind of ready for you not to be on the best-seller list anymore."

"You are?" I asked.

"So you'll stay home again."

I winced just a little and promised her I'm getting better at saying no. Then I reminded her we were like surfers riding a dizzyingly giant wave.

"It's a crazy ride, honey," I said, snugging the blanket around her. "But soon enough we'll be back on shore."

*July 17, 2006*

# A Trek to the North Pole, for His One True Friend

Sometimes a dog is more than a pet.

It can be a joy in good times, a comfort in bad, an un-questioning friend always. The special ones can change a person's life. A very few might just land you at the North Pole.

For Barry Greenberg, that dog was Kunitz.

For 11 years, the powerful, intelligent Siberian husky was at Greenberg's side through the ups and downs of life. Kunitz was there through a divorce and through career changes. He was there as his owner started over and found love again.

For much of Kunitz's life, Greenberg, who now resides in Quebec, lived in Wilmington and worked in West Chester as a biotechnology researcher.

Greenberg had never been one to celebrate winter, but the snow-loving animal of proud Arctic heritage changed that. Greenberg began hiking daily with him in Brandywine Creek State Park near his home and soon caught what he called his dog's "winter lust."

It didn't take long for the Alzheimer's disease researcher to begin dreaming of what huskies live to do: pull heavy loads across frozen landscapes of white.

Greenberg took his first dogsledding expedition in northern Minnesota in 1996, when he was 40. Seven more trips would follow—and his second marriage would take place on the back of a dogsled in the middle of a frozen Minnesota landscape.

"Kunitz," he told me last week, "was my best friend for a very long time, with me through some of life's great trials."

In 2002, while Greenberg was in Sweden at a conference, the call came from home in Wilmington that his beloved husky had suffered a seizure and died. "I never had the chance to say goodbye," he said.

Greenberg spread some of Kunitz's ashes in the state park where the husky loved to romp. But he saved a small amount with a special dream in mind—to one day travel by dogsled to the top of the Earth and release them on vast ice cap where huskies' spirits never die.

In April of this year, Greenberg's dream became a reality. He joined an expedition led by his dogsledding mentor Paul Schurke, the veteran Arctic adventurer. The group flew to Norway, where it outfitted itself with dogs, sleds, and supplies. Then it flew to a Russian research camp one degree from the North Pole. The group then flew by helicopter with the trained sled dogs, sleds, and supplies to a point about 120 miles from the pole and set out on an arduous 11-day passage. With temperatures hovering well below zero degrees Fahrenheit the entire trip, the expedition braved strong winds, steep ice ridges, open water, and treacherous soft ice.

At the end of each day, the group of nine, with four sleds and 32 dogs, slept in tents on the ice.

In his backpack, Greenberg carried Kunitz's leather collar and a small plastic vial of the dog's ashes. On the final day, April 25, he lashed the collar to the outside of his pack, and the tags jingled as he walked, giving him an odd sense of peace, as if Kunitz were there walking beside him.

The group arrived at the North Pole at 6 p.m., and almost immediately Greenberg set about the task for which he had come. He walked a few paces from his cohorts, dropped to his knee, and used a knife to break the seal on the container. Almost instantly, he said, a strong gust of wind carried the fine ashes off.

"I'm keeping my promise to you, Kunitz," he whispered, "You were a good boy. You always will be."

And then he thanked him. For the companionship and loyalty, the intuition and canine empathy. For the goofy way he howled along whenever he heard people singing "Happy Birthday" but no other songs.

He thanked the dog for helping him find a new life and a new wife and for setting him on the path to the adventure of a lifetime.

In the subzero Arctic air, unanticipated tears welling in his eyes, he saw it all so clearly, the way an animal can enrich and deepen the human experience, often in mysterious and unexpected ways.

"Thank you, Kunitz," he said.

*October 2, 2006*

## Alpha Bet: It'll Work on Lids, Too
### *A Household of Dysfunctional Dog Owners Heels to the Will of the Whisperer*

When my wife, Jenny, told me the Dog Whisperer would be coming to our home to help us become better pet parents, I admit I rolled my eyes.

I am a plenty fine pet parent. My pets run all over me, and I put up with it. You got a problem with that?

Regardless, it seemed this whisperer guy was arriving a little too late.

After all, our famously bad-boy Labrador retriever, Marley, shredder of couches and flinger of drool, had long ago departed for that great obedience school in the sky.

His replacement, a shy, sedate female named Gracie, is so good she is boring.

"Um, is there something he needs to whisper to me?" I asked.

Cesar Millan came to this country from Mexico and slowly built a reputation for his ability to turn around even the most problematic and disturbed dogs. Today, he hosts the popular television show *Dog Whisperer* on the National Geographic Channel, and his dog-behavior book, *Cesar's Way*, is a best-seller.

His big message is that it's usually not the dogs that need attitude adjustments, but their human handlers. Dogs, like a lot of humans, are natural-born followers, but they will only line up behind a strong, confident leader. Think Roosevelt after Pearl Harbor or Giuliani after 9/11.

Millan's mission in life is to instill these elusive leadership qualities in dog owners. He calls it "calm assertiveness." True leaders, he argues, don't yell or shout or lose their cool; they calmly and quietly assert their will on others.

Not in our house. Our animals are under the impression they live in a democracy, and they have an equal vote.

One day after watching his show, Jenny had one of those "why not" moments and e-mailed Millan's producers. Of course, they loved the idea of America's best-known dog behaviorist taking on what may very well now be its best-known dysfunctional-dog owners. (My parents would be so proud.) Or as they put it, "that Marley family."

Last week, Millan and his seven-person television crew arrived for their second of two visits.

During the first visit in August, Millan observed that Gracie, while naturally pretty well behaved, was adrift, trying to find her own way in the world without benefit of a clear pack leader.

"You have her trust and affection," he said, "but not her respect."

Hey, just like my children!

Within minutes, and without ever raising his hand or voice, he had Gracie bowing to him in supplication. He spent most of his time training us to exert alpha assertiveness. Our dog just looked at me as if to say, if you're the pack leader, I'm Madonna.

By the time Millan returned last week, Gracie seemed to treat us with new respect. She came when we called her, and sat at the door awaiting our permission before barging out. The Dog Whisperer was pleased.

The more Millan talked about surefire methods to control dogs, and to earn their respect, the more I kept thinking: Forget the dumb dog; I'm trying this out on the kids!

As parents, we can't put shock collars on our children and zap them every time they misbehave, but what if we used some of the same techniques Millan uses on animals?

What if we applied these commonsense techniques of calm, assertive leadership? What if we forgot about being our sons' and daughters' pals and instead focused on being their . . . parents?

Over a beer at the end of the day, I only half-joked, "Will you come live with us and be our Teen Whisperer?"

Millan laughed, then volunteered that he receives a steady stream of letter and e-mails from parents requesting just that.

With his own sons, 12 and 7, he said he follows a similar philosophy. He gives them lots of chores and exercise to burn off excess energy, and tries not to inadvertently reward bad behavior—even when it's cute.

He thinks twice before issuing an edict. Once issued, there is no room for self-doubt. Kids, like dogs, have a radar for weakness and will exploit it.

And as with dogs, he believes one firm, memorable correction is worth a thousand idle threats. In other words, when you say no, you better mean it. And follow through.

Dogs are easy to figure out; kids, especially your own, quite another matter. And yet, as Millan and his entourage pulled out of the driveway, I felt oddly empowered on both counts.

Gracie looked at me as if to say, "Good riddance! Now we can get back to normal." My three children seemed to be having the same thought.

I leveled my gaze on the dog, then on the kids, and practiced my best look of quiet confidence. I could almost hear Cesar whisper: Believe in yourself and they will believe, too.

"Not so fast," I said.

*December 29, 2006*

# Skip the Gun,
# Try Four-Legged Security

When the kidnapper slipped into 8-year-old Laura Staples's bedroom on that Sunday night in 1998, he failed to consider one important point.

The Stapleses' Hatboro home was armed with a power-ful secret weapon hardwired to prevent just such a crime. A weapon at once potentially deadly but guaranteed to never accidentally harm a family member.

The weapon was not a handgun or assault rifle or how-itzer. It didn't answer to the name of Glock or Colt or Ruger.

It answered to the name of Rocky. And it was 120 pounds of finely tuned, rippling-muscled Rhodesian ridge-back dog.

The intruder flashed a knife and cupped his hand over Laura's mouth as her parents, Michael and Joan, slept in the next room. "She gave it her best fight, but the creep got the upper hand and started down the stairs with her," her father recalled last week.

As the girl struggled helplessly against him, her foot knocked a picture off the wall.

The noise was not enough to rouse her parents, but it did awaken Rocky, who had been sleeping on the third floor—where he wasn't supposed to be—with Laura's older sister, Megan.

The dog charged down the stairs, teeth bared, and lunged. "The bad guy tried to use Laura as a shield, but Rocky was too smart for that," Mike Staples recounted. "He bit the bastard wherever he could."

### Irrefutable Evidence

The intruder dropped Laura and ran for the door. Rocky chased him down and clamped his powerful jaws over the man's forearm, leaving a gruesome wound that forensic experts would later use to tie a suspect arrested nearby to the crime.

By now, Laura's screams filled the house, and her father ran downstairs brandishing a loaded handgun he kept in the house for self-defense. The bad man was already gone, and it was a good thing, Staples realized.

His adrenaline was pumping, heart pounding, temples throbbing. Screams filled the air. Confusion reigned. In mere seconds, from a dead sleep, he was trying to process an aborted crime that could have shattered his family forever. Staples, an experienced hunter and shooting enthusiast, was in no shape to be making life-or-death decisions with a loaded weapon.

"I was out of body. I wasn't Mike Staples. I was Hulk Hogan suddenly. I would have had no problem blowing someone's brains out," the father said.

To this day, it unnerves him to think what might have happened had he, not Rocky, confronted the kidnapper on the stairs, he holding a gun, the bad guy holding Laura.

"Had I been in the mix with the gun, bad things could have happened," he said. "When you have a 120-pound dog charging down the stairs at you, there are no hostage negotiations."

### Eternally Grateful

Eight years have passed since that horrible night. Frankie Burton, a convicted child molester, was convicted in the kidnapping attempt and sent to prison for 42 to 118 years. Laura is 16 now, a junior at Hatboro-Horsham High School, where she runs cross-country. With the help of years of therapy, the psychological wounds are slowly washing away.

Rocky, an incorrigible bad boy who more than once was brought home in the backseat of a police car after breaking loose to romance the female canines of Hatboro, got steak dinners, a parade, and the 2000 National Dog Hero Award, given by the Society for the Prevention of Cruelty to Animals Los Angeles.

More importantly, he earned his family's eternal gratitude.

Three years ago, veterinarians diagnosed cancer in Rocky. He died on May 12, 2004, on the night before his ninth birthday. "The sense of loss, it was unfathomable," Staples said. "This dog saved our family. There are no words to express the emotion or the pain."

The Stapleses have a new bad-boy dog now. His name is Junior, and he can often be found sleeping at Laura's feet.

Staples is a sportsman who is comfortable around guns. But he thinks his family's experience serves as a good lesson for anyone considering buying a weapon for home protection.

"I've thought about the gun thing a lot," he said. "After the bad guy, I just locked mine up. Guns don't work in the house. A dog is really the best thing. Which is why I tell everyone I know, don't get a gun, get a dog."

*Life*

# New Scribe:
# A Suburbanite Geek

Hey there. I'm the new guy. New to *The Inquirer*, sort of new to the area, and with a new column that will appear here three times a week, focusing on the Pennsylvania suburbs.

Yeah, I'm one of those geeky suburbanites. When all my cool friends are attending Center City art openings in their black Gap tees, I'm out crawling around my front lawn worrying about the dandelions.

And yes, shame of shame, there's a minivan parked in my garage.

My kids are always throwing these ridiculous propositions at me. The other day, the 9-year-old said: "Dad, if you won $10 million and could only spend it in one store, what would it be?"

I thought. And I thought. And the only place I could think of was . . . Home Depot. Pathetic.

You want to know how I spent a recent weekend? Building a tree fort. And I'm terrified of heights. I'm 18 feet up in the air in a swaying—swaying!—tree. I'm trying to hammer nails while holding on with a white-knuckle death grip. The kids went inside hours ago. Why am I up here?

And why not the *Bulletin*?

My bosses want me to introduce myself to you. What can I say? My dad grew up in Philadelphia's Germantown section a block off Chelten Avenue. He still talks about swimming in the Wissahickon Creek. When I told him I got this job, he said, "*The Inquirer*? Why not the *Bulletin*? That's the big-name paper in town."

Uh, Dad, how can I break this to you?

By the time I came along, we were in Detroit, which is kind of like Philadelphia without the nice parts. I was born on 8 Mile Road, right where rapper Eminem's new movie was filmed. It would make a great story to tell you Em and I hung in the 'hood together, but age-wise I'm closer to Chaucer. And by the time I was potty-trained, my life in the 'burbs had begun.

Journalism jobs took me from Michigan to Ohio to Florida and, three years ago, to southeastern Pennsylvania where I was editor of a gardening magazine. (You can call there only if you promise not to ask me about your crabgrass.)

The last few weeks I've been wandering around the region a lot. Man, is this place old. The cemeteries are all filled with Revolutionary War veterans. Of course, South Florida, where I spent 12 years, six of them as a newspaper columnist, has plenty of Revolutionary War vets, too; the difference is, they're still driving.

This whole place is like a Smithsonian exhibit. Is there anywhere George Washington didn't sleep?

I was in New Hope the other night. As far as I can tell, the newest thing in New Hope is about 200 years old. If this is New Hope, what is the Old Hope? I guess that would be Bob.

I see the region's helpful developers are doing their part to make sure there's plenty of new, too. If Philadelphia is ever invaded, we can rest easy knowing we've fortified the perimeter with Wawas and T.G.I. Friday's.

### Everybody Loves William

But it's the historic stuff that has me smitten. I keep meeting people who insist their homes were originally deeded three centuries ago by William Penn. Either that or by Penn's old college roommate, Sir Frank Lautenberg. (There I go exaggerating again. Frank actually bunked with Lincoln.)

What is the big deal about William Penn, anyway?

And why is everything named after him? I landed here, too—hauling three goldfish, two frogs, and a heavily sedated Labrador retriever, no less—and I don't see anyone naming the waterfront Grogan's Landing.

History is so plentiful around here, it's almost cheap. The auto-parts store near my house is in an ancient farmhouse that in most places would be a museum. The corner tavern claims to be in its 267th year of continuous service—and, trust me, the bathrooms are still waiting for their first cleaning.

I can't wait to jump in on the local issues. There are some real doozies.

This whole listeria thing has me freaked out. I've got listeria hysteria.

The other day, after reading about the latest recall, I screamed at my wife: "For God's sake! I gargle with that stuff every day!"

"That's Listerine," she said. "Grogan, you're an idiot."

Listerine, listeria, Liz Taylor. Whatever.

*December 24, 2002*

# Spreading Cheer
## the Interfaith Way

A few nights ago, I went in search of true Christmas spirit. Guess where I found it? On the second level of the King of Prussia Mall, right in front of the J. C. Penney entrance.

I found it at a counter lined with wrapping paper, ribbons, and little Jewish ladies.

The women—and a couple of their husbands—cut, folded, tucked, and taped at a furious pace, turning mall purchases into Christmas gifts.

They did it without pay for a holiday they don't celebrate. They did it with cheer and smiles, despite hours on their feet.

They did it as a mitzvah—a good deed to the community. Not only were they helping harried shoppers—most of them wrapping-impaired guys like me—with each gift, they where helping those less fortunate.

As chief gift-wrapper Sandy Heitner put it: "Not one penny goes to any of us. All the money is donated to charity."

The shoppers happily fork over anywhere from $1 to $8 a gift, depending on size, for the service. Many toss in generous tips. One man handed the women a $20 bill for a $6 wrap, and said, "Keep the change."

Even the tips are donated.

The money will go to local police officers for bullet-proof vests, to firefighters for hoses, to local libraries, to senior centers, and to the Red Cross. A local ambulance squad will get a chunk. So will Upper Merion High School and the homeless of Montgomery County.

## A Pint-Size Dynamo

Heitner, a pint-size dynamo with bifocals perched on her nose, and her husband, Jerry, have been working on the annual wrapping project since October, when they began putting out calls for volunteers. Acting under the auspices of the Jewish service group B'nai B'rith, the couple hopes to raise more then $10,000 by the time the booth closes tonight.

"It's just like a little store," she says. "It has to run smoothly. We have these last-minute customers who want their gifts wrapped."

And on my night there, the shoppers lined up with bas-ketballs and lamps, mirrors and nightgowns, waiting for the volunteers to work their magic. As one who has been there, I could feel the shoppers' relief. A guy named Milton looked at me and said simply, "Worth every penny."

Third-year volunteer wrapper Linda Halpern of Conshohocken finds the hapless men amusing, especially the dad who, amid the luxury shops of King of Prussia, asked her, "So, where can I find the dollar store?"

Standing beside Halpern was Dan Gross, a retired orthopedic surgeon from Chesterbrook, wrapping a gift with surgical precision—but no sutures. "I'll try anything," he said. And the free coffee donated by a food-court vender isn't bad, either, he said.

### Intense Couple of Weeks

The mall donates the space for the wrapping counter, and an Allentown company provides discount paper, boxes, and bows. Each night after the booth closes, the Heitners tally the day's take, restock the cupboards, then get on the phone to line up the next day's volunteers, not all of whom are Jewish.

"It is a two and a half week period that is very intense," Sandy Heitner said.

Why do they do it? Why fight the mall crowds each day to wrap gifts for strangers when they can be curled up in front of the fireplace back home in West Norriton?

Jerry Heitner said it was to remind those who celebrate Christmas that their Jewish neighbors "are positive, contributing members of the community." His wife said it is simply for the good feeling of doing good.

Volunteer Chele Leyva of Chesterbrook, talking as she spliced paper together to cover a giant karaoke machine, said there's something about the wrapping table that brings out the best in wrappers and shoppers alike.

"You have moments when you ask yourself, 'Why am I doing this?' But, mostly, it's fun," she said. "It's the happy side of Christmas. People are just so glad you're doing this. They're not yelling at you for cutting in line."

Actually, it's much more than the happy side. It's the real and meaningful side. A side where people of different faiths come together in selfless good cheer to help each other. It's a side we could all use a little more of.

*December 27, 2002*

## Weather to Croon and Swoon Over

I have been waiting half my life for a white Christmas. On Wednesday, I finally got one.

Bing Crosby, eat your heart out.

True, 12 of my last 15 years were spent in Florida, where the only white stuff hitting the ground was coming from the drug couriers' duffel bags.

But for years before moving to Florida, I saw no Christmas snow. And after returning north to Pennsylvania three years ago, I still saw none. The last Christmas here to have even a dusting was in 1998.

At dawn I awakened to the roar of stampeding hooves in the hallway. Either Rudolph and his team had taken a wrong turn or my kids were up.

"Daddy!" the 5-year-old shrieked. "Santa made it snow!"

"Great. Go back to bed."

As if that was going to happen.

She yanked open the blinds. Outside stretched a vast canvas of white.

Wow. I was awake.

Being older and wiser, I knew Santa played no role at all. The real reason was that two days earlier I had finally washed the salt off my car, which pretty much guaranteed a major storm.

Different parts of the region got different amounts, anywhere from a dusting to a dumping. In my microclimate, up on suburbia's brave northern frontier, big wet flakes kept falling all day. By the time the smell of roasting turkey filled the house, seven inches had piled up on the deck.

### Snow Driving Wimps

Everyone was bailing on holiday dinner plans. The roads were just too treacherous. May I say that we've all become a bunch of winter-driving wimps. Back when I was a kid, a little blizzard never stopped anyone. We'd just crank up the Model T and off we'd go, a shotgun in the back window in case we needed provisions along the way. Now, a hint of frost brings traffic to a screeching halt.

Not that I was complaining. When it comes to relatives and holidays, I'm firmly in the "less is more" camp.

My bachelor brother managed to make it in from New Jersey, bearing gifts of dirty laundry for our washing machine. We call him Uncle Buck.

As the snow piled up, my kids were so ecstatic they raced to the computer to play virtual video snowboarding.

"You guys, hello?" I said. "You can do the real thing outside, you know."

No response. Not even a glimmer.

"Hello? Can anyone hear me?"

Am I the only father in America who comes with a mute button?

Eventually, I got their attention and got them outside—after earning my Ph.D. in snowsuit zipperology. The kids had fun playing the Let's Stuff Ice Down Dad's Shirt game.

The soggy snow was perfect for packing, and soon we were building a fort that could have stopped a Humvee. One by one, the kids retreated to the house for hot chocolate. Eventually it was just Uncle Buck and me. Two grown men on their knees in the snow, working away to keep the home front safe from enemy snowball attack.

When was the last time we had played in the snow together? I'm pretty sure Lyndon Johnson was still president. I looked at my brother through the falling snow and saw someone I had not seen for decades—the 12-year-old boy I had once shared a bedroom with. There was only one thing to do: Wind up and nail him with a snowball.

### Surprise Dinner Guests

My neighbor Steve pulled up with his snowplow. He and his wife and kids were supposed to be driving to Lower

Bucks for Christmas dinner at the in-laws'. Not in this, they decided.

We had a turkey and no one to eat with. They had wine and no one to toast with. Besides, the guy had just plowed my driveway.

So dinner it was, two families thrown together by the whimsy of a winter storm that happened to arrive on a day we call Christmas.

I whipped up my nearly famous gravy. My wife mashed a few extra potatoes. Uncle Buck spiked the eggnog. And we had an impromptu party. No expectations, no baggage, no stress.

After dinner, the kids played in the basement while the adults assembled toys. Outside, the storm had stopped, ensconcing our little world in a pure cocoon of white. Peace on Earth.

Who knows? Maybe my daughter was right. Maybe Santa did bring the snow—a simple gift of joy and tranquility to a rushed and cynical world.

*January 3, 2003*

## Boob Eyes Tube While Driving

It's 5:20 p.m. on a workday, and I am merging onto the Vine Street Expressway into a wall of traffic. In front of me, a Ford Escort that looks like an escapee from the salvage yard weaves like a bee.

A weaving car in Philly rush hour? Stop the presses! But this car catches my eye. The passenger compartment emanates an odd blue-gray glow, the kind of otherworldly radiance you might see coming from a spaceship just before aliens emerge and ask to see your leader. (What? You mean, you've never seen this?)

The glow gets the best of my curiosity. I slip between two tractor-trailer rigs and pull alongside. This is what I see: A man watching television.

Not a passenger watching TV. The driver watching TV. As he merges into traffic. At the height of rush hour.

Earth to aliens: Beam him up, please.

The TV is not some miniature travel model. It's the real deal, the kind you might have on your kitchen counter.

And it's somehow wedged on the dashboard above the center console where it blocks the better part of the windshield.

## Survivor: The Sequel

In my commuting adventures, I have seen a lot: drivers shaving, applying makeup, tying ties, reading novels, jotting notes, and, of course, gabbing endlessly on cell phones. I've even seen motorists executing several of these multitasking feats of skill simultaneously.

But never before have I seen someone turn a car into a mobile multiplex. What? No Raisinets?

I'm dying to find out what could be such must-see TV that this upstanding member of the commuting public would risk his life and everyone else's around him to watch.

Couldn't he wait till he was in safer surrounding—say, while dismantling explosives back in his garage—to tune in? I pull beside him again and can almost see what's on the screen when—WHOA! Here he comes!

I hit the brakes. The truck behind me hits the brakes. The 13,000 commuters behind the truck hit their brakes. And over drifts Mr. Teletubby. No blinker. No warning. No clue.

I back off and follow at a safe distance, watching the glowing Escort wind and weave up the Schuylkill and onto the Blue Route. I finally lose him at Plymouth Meeting when he peels off on 276 East toward New Jersey.

Where is Tony Soprano when we need him?

I never did find out what my pal was watching. But I'm pretty sure he had his own private Ralph and Norton show unfolding right there in the driver's seat.

If he keeps this up, he's sure to get his very own show: *Do You Want to Be a Highway Smear?*

## Crime and Punishment

Later, I talk to State Police Trooper Chris Paris at the Belmont Barracks. This can't be legal, can it?

Trooper Paris assures me that driving under the influence of reruns is definitely not legal. Specifically, Title 75, section 4527 of the Pennsylvania Vehicle Code prohibits any motor vehicle from having a television mounted "forward of the back of the driver's seat or otherwise visible to the driver."

"If I saw that on the road, I'd pull him over and write him a ticket," Paris said. Yes!

And the fine? A whopping $25 ($100 with costs).

Well, it's the thought that counts.

Trooper Paris wants to stress that looking away for even a moment—let alone for a half-hour sitcom—can be deadly. And more of us, he says, are looking away—to dial cell phones, to eat Big Macs, and, in my case, to try to figure out what the guy in the next car is watching.

"At 55 mph, you're traveling 80 feet per second. That's the physics of it. And who drives 55 out there?"

No one I know. Anything else?

"Any task that takes away from the driving is a potentially dangerous one."

OK, trooper, are you about done?

"You are your neighbor's keeper. By driving carelessly, not only do you hazard yourself, but you put everyone else at risk."

So is this guy a complete moron?

"I would say unwise."

Trooper, you're kinder than I am.

OK, Mr. Unwise, here's a tip: next time you hear the boob tube's siren call, do us all a favor. Pull over.

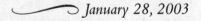 *January 28, 2003*

# Ditch the Speedo, and Other Fla. Tips

Look! Up in the sky! What's that blotting out the sun? Is it a plane? Is it a blimp? Is it a flock of jumbo-sized Canada geese?

No, it's just the annual migration of the Great Northern Pale-Bellied Snowbirds as they flock from their home range in the Philadelphia region to the fabled winter thawing grounds of South Florida. Caw! Caw! Caw!

With the temperatures in the Northeast dancing into the single digits, the southward stream of half-frozen pale-bellies has reached a frenzied pace.

The signs are everywhere: darkened houses, boarded pets, piled-up mail, empty offices. Have you tried to find long-term parking at the airport lately?

The featherless snowbirds are heading south en masse, some for a few days, some till spring, and I only have one question: Will the last one out please leave me his long johns?

Unlike most migratory birds, the Great Northern Pale-Bellied Snowbird is not protected under federal law, which makes sense, I guess, considering it's the only known avian to fly coach class wearing loud clothing.

I spent 12 years living at ground zero of the annual invasion—Palm Beach County—observing the pale-bellies interact, often disastrously, with the native species. I went to help.

Here's the first thing snowbirds need to know before taking flight: Floridians will smile as they take your money, but make no mistake, they're laughing at you behind your back. Snowbird character assassination is a favorite pastime in the Sunshine State—and there's no bag limit.

The second thing snowbirds need to know is, balmy skies and white sand aside, it's a jungle down there. This is a place where the T-shirts read: "Don't shoot; I live here!"

So I've put together these Snowbird Survival Tips to help my migratory neighbors avoid harm and ridicule while thawing out:

**Leave the Speedo at home.** I know it looked buff on you back when you where training with Mark Spitz, but time marches on. Snowbirds tend to follow the inverse rule: the larger the body, the smaller the suit. Buck the trend and cover up.

**Try not to fry.** Too many snowbirds assume the vacation is a bomb unless they return home sporting third-degree sunburn. The lobster look is a sure giveaway you're a Great Northern fly-in. Floridians spend years perfecting their skin cancer; don't try to catch up in a week.

**Steer clear of seniors.** South Florida's large elderly population looks harmless enough, but don't be fooled. I've witnessed seniors duke it out over parking spaces. In November, a 74-year-old man died from a head injury after he was slugged during a scuffle in line for movie tickets. The suspect: a 68-year-old.

**Don't become roadkill.** Along those same lines, my advice is to stay off the roads. You think Philly drivers are out of control? We're a bunch of Mario Andrettis compared to Florida drivers, many of whom haven't had a vision test since Grover Cleveland was president. I've seen drivers plow their cars into swimming pools, store windows, fire hydrants, you name it. Mr. Magoo lives—and he drives a Buick in Delray Beach.

**Speak like a local.** Boca Raton, where I used to live, is pretty high on itself (probably because it has more face-lifts per capita than any other place on earth). Pronounce the town wrong and you are marked for life. So repeat after me: Boca Ruh-TONE. Not ruh-tahhn. Not ruh-tan. Ruh-tone. If you really want to impress the locals, simply say, "Bowh-ka!"

**Drop the fib.** Don't call your long-lost relation in Fort Lauderdale and say, "I've really missed you, Cuz." He'll see right through it. All Floridians have had this scam pulled on them. If you want to show your Florida kin you love them, visit in August. If you want a free place to stay in February, try the homeless shelter.

**Don't get lured by the early bird.** That great Florida institution, the early-bird special, offers really bad food at ungodly hours for unbelievably low prices. The locals avoid these joints like typhoid. If you want to blend in, you should, too.

Now go have fun in the sun.

As for me, I'll be ice fishing.

*February 4, 2003*

# 9/11 Altered Our View of Tragedy

On Saturday morning I was in a high school cafeteria with 200 other parents from across Southeastern Pennsylvania, receiving judge training for a regional student competition.

About 9:30, a man with a cell phone in his hand broke in, whispered something to the speaker, and then announced in a loud voice, "The space shuttle *Columbia* apparently has just broken up over Texas."

At that moment, I realized just how much September 11, 2001, has changed us.

Two hundred people in a room, and this is what we did: Collectively, momentarily, reeled back. Sucked in a sharp, short breath. Blinked hard.

A few gasped. One man in back asked for the information to be repeated. Another asked how many were aboard. A woman said, "Oh my God."

And that was it. We returned to our meeting as if nothing had happened. Our collective shock and grief lasted all of 90 seconds.

Flash back 17 years and four days. January 28, 1986. I was a graduate assistant at Ohio State University, teaching editing to a classroom full of second-year journalism students.

The door opened and a young woman from the student newspaper across the hall burst in, visibly shaken. "The space shuttle just exploded," she blurted out.

The television went on, the now-famous images of those errant white plumes in the blue Atlantic sky playing over and over. Hands covered mouths, eyes welled with tears, faces turned ashen. We stood frozen for hours, and our lives remained in lockdown for days as the nation reeled with shock and grief.

## A Changed Landscape

Sitting with those other parents Saturday, the sense of *déjà vu* was palpable. And yet, something was jarringly different.

I was surprised—and slightly appalled—at how quickly we processed the tragedy, compartmentalized it, and moved on.

What had taken us weeks to work through after *Challenger* took us less than two minutes. Not another word was spoken about it for the rest of the morning. Speakers got up and sat down, presentations were made, handouts distributed, questions asked.

It was as if *Columbia* had not really been lost. As if what had been described to us was just a scene from a reality TV show. Real but not really real.

Our ambivalence surprised but did not shock me. In the wake of 9/11, the explosion of a space shuttle by no nefarious design was tragic, certainly, but somehow less so than what we all now know is possible.

I'm ashamed to admit that almost instantly I worked the numbers. Seven lost. Seven lives, seven of our best and brightest. Heroes, gone in a flash. Horribly sad. And yet.

Seven is not 700. Or 7,000.

And yet.

A fatal mishap in the netherworld of Earth's outer atmosphere in a pursuit as inherently risky as space travel is not terrorists striking ordinary Americans as they go about the routines of their daily lives.

## A Scale of Tragedy

And yet.

Death by nature's fury is not death by the hand of human hatred.

On the post–9/11 national-tragedy scale, this one, mercifully, fell somewhere less than a 10. That is not to minimize the loss, searing and profound, but rather to acknowledge the context.

We have changed. Our nation has changed. We are tougher now, harder. Our hearts are no less big, but the innocence—that optimism and blind belief in goodness we Americans are so famous for—is tempered.

We have been reminded—in horrible ways—that this world is a dangerous, unpredictable place, and death can come at anytime to anyone.

On Saturday night as I watched the *Columbia* tragedy unfold on CNN, an announcer broke in with yet another reminder of life's fragility: Seven high school students, children not unlike yours or mine, were buried by an avalanche in British Columbia. Seven more bright stars extinguished.

I reeled back. Sucked in a sharp, short breath. Blinked hard. Then moved on.

*February 10, 2003*

## Her Shop Corners
## Market on Dignity

On the matter of breast cancer, Marguerite Spina tells her customers, "I've been there, done that."

Thirteen years ago, she was a West Chester wife, a mom, an auto insurance claims adjuster chugging happily through life.

Then she found the lump. "That's what got the ball rolling," she says. It rolled her out of an ordinary life and into a place no one wants to enter—a world of doctors and hospitals, chemotherapy, and surgery.

Before it was over, she lost her hair. She lost her left breast. And when it was time to pick up the pieces and carry on, she nearly lost her dignity as well.

That's the part that sticks with her all these years later— the humiliating ordeal of having to find a wig to cover her bald head and a silicone breast form to fill the empty spot beneath her blouse. The sales clerks were uncomfortable with her, which made her uncomfortable with herself.

One day she found herself alone in a storage room at a pharmacy, facing a wall full of boxes. It was up to her to sort through them to find an artificial breast that would fit her.

She decided right then that this was not right. And she began to dream of a store that specialized in just one thing: helping women navigate the frightful world of breast cancer with their dignity intact.

## A Better Place to Go

"Women needed a better place to go where they wouldn't be treated like second-class citizens," she says.

Now a ruddy-cheeked, 58-year-old grandmother, Spina has realized her dream. She owns the Yellow Daffodils Wig Salon & Post Mastectomy Boutique at 961 Downingtown Pike. With a name like that, you can bet it doesn't get many walk-ins.

Her customers arrive by word of mouth from doctors and other breast-cancer survivors. They come from all around. One woman drove all the way from Long Beach Island, New Jersey.

The shop is in a converted farmhouse between West Chester and Downingtown. Open the door and it's like stumbling into someone's family room, complete with wicker furniture and fresh flowers.

Four of the seven women who work there are cancer survivors themselves.

"It's not a job requirement," Spina says. "It just worked out that way."

The women try to keep the mood light and upbeat as they fit customers with wigs, hats, undergarments, and artificial breasts. "I've had people say, 'This is the first time I've laughed since this all began,'" Spina says.

But it can be a bleak business.

Her customers have been as young as 12. Just last month, a 17-year-old with flowing hair was in to buy a wig in anticipation of her chemotherapy. Most of the women are in their 40s and 50s.

"You have a lot of women come in here who you know aren't going to make it," she says.

### Sadness and Satisfaction

They are the ones you don't soon forget. A woman with a brain tumor came for a wig. She told Spina the doctors had given her two options: take no treatment and live 90 days or undergo radiation and last six months.

"I never saw her again," Spina says.

And here at Yellow Daffodils, the bell can toll close to home. Kim Ledgerwood beat cancer several years ago and spent the last four years working at the store, where she become a beloved member of the staff.

Then the cancer returned. "She fought it for a little over a year," Spina says. "It just kept spreading."

Her friend died three weeks ago. She was 46 and left behind a husband and two sons.

Spina and the other women who work here balance the sadness with the satisfaction of knowing they are helping women at a most vulnerable time. There is no charge for the empathy, listening, and hugs.

"We've been in their shoes," she says. "It's kind of a buddy system."

Averaging just 10 customers a week, Spina doesn't make a lot of money at this. "It pays the rent most months," she says.

But money is not why she is here.

She is here to stand as a beacon of hope for women navigating the darkest passage of their lives. Her very presence beams a needed message: "We survived it, and so can you."

*February 11, 2003*

## Taking a Shot at Buying a Gun

"I want to buy a shotgun," I said.

The young man at the Wal-Mart sporting-goods counter didn't miss a beat. "What did you have in mind?" he asked, unlocking the gun case.

His name was Bob, and he sported bleached hair and baggy, low-slung pants. I asked to see the cheapest shotgun he had. Bob pulled out a single-shot, 20-gauge New England brand with a price tag of $85.

Such a deal. I had come prepared to spend a few hundred.

Bob placed it in my hands. I didn't try to hide my ignorance. "How do you load this thing?" I asked.

He showed me how to break open the barrel, slide in a shell, click it shut. "Then you're set to go," Bob said.

I had come to this Wal-Mart near Quakertown, in Upper Bucks County, as a customer to see just how easy—and fast—it was to buy a weapon.

What brought me here was the suicide of Richard Lee of Willow Grove.

On February 2, police say, Lee, 25, walked into a Wal-Mart in Horsham and, after passing an instant background check, bought a 20-gauge shotgun. He then drove to a Wal-Mart in Warminster, where he bought shells.

From there, he drove directly to Cavalier Telephone in Warminster, which had laid him off, and began firing. The final round, police say, was for himself.

Blessedly, no one was present for the Sunday night rampage, and Lee was the only casualty. But it doesn't take much imagination to picture what could have been had he arrived during work hours.

### No Hard Questions

And so on Friday I went to Wal-Mart to experience first-hand the safeguards that failed to save Richard Lee from himself. I sighted briefly down the barrel then said, "OK, I'll take it." I had been at the counter for four minutes.

I was waiting for Bob to grill me about my inexperience and motives for wanting a cheap gun. Had I completed a gun-safety course? Did I have any practice handling firearms?

Instead he asked me for two pieces of identification and gave me a federal form that asked a series of yes/no questions intended to root out the unstable and criminally inclined.

Had I ever been convicted of a felony? Ever been the subject of a restraining order? Any history of domestic abuse? Mental illness? Drunken driving? Drug addiction?

If I had evil intent, did they really expect me to answer truthfully?

I handed Bob $2 for the background check and he phoned in my information to the state police's Pennsylvania Instant Check database.

Ten minutes later, he returned with a box and packed my shotgun into it.

"Does this mean I passed?" I asked.

"Yep. No problem," Bob said.

I asked if I could buy shells for the shotgun, too. Bob apologized and said store policy did not allow that.

We wouldn't want people to start shooting until they were safely out of the store now, would we? If the ammunition restriction was meant as a deterrent, it wasn't much of one. There was a Kmart across the street that sold ammunition.

### On Second Thought

Bob rang up my sale, and I reached for my credit card. Once I paid, I was free to walk out with my new weapon.

But I didn't really want this weapon, and at Wal-Mart, as with other gun shops I checked, all gun sales are final. No returns; no exchanges.

And so at the last second, with apologies to Bob for wasting his time, I pulled the plug on my little experiment and walked out of the store empty-handed. The entire process had taken 27 minutes.

Just for kicks, I drove across Route 309, walked into Kmart and bought a box of 25 Winchester Super-X gameload shells for $3.79. No ID required; no questions asked.

On the way home, I wasn't feeling particularly homicidal or suicidal or deranged. But had I been—and had I not aborted my shotgun sale at the last moment—I would have been, in Bob's words, "set to go."

I later checked with the state police in Harrisburg, who confirmed that Bob had properly done everything the law asks of him. Pennsylvania requires no gun-safety training. No proof of competence. No cooling-off period. Not even an overnight delay. Just 27 minutes and two forms of ID.

That wasn't enough to stop Richard Lee. And it won't be enough to stop the next Richard Lee, either.

*February 21, 2003*

## Tired of Sales Calls? Try Defense Tactics

Most of us agree that telemarketers are among the lower life forms on the planet, falling somewhere between mold and fungi. The only difference is they have better speed-dialing skills.

They call at dinnertime, selling time-shares. On Sunday, selling credit cards. After a birth, selling college funds. After a death, selling crypts.

They call. They call. They call.

Government is trying to protect us, but, let's face it, the laws of a civilized society don't mean much to lower life forms. Since Pennsylvania's "Do Not Call" law went into effect November 1, the state attorney general has received more than 3,000 complaints from people who are still getting pestered despite being on the no-calls registry.

You might as well politely ask cockroaches to please not trespass into your cupboard. Sometimes you just need to reach for the Raid.

I don't lightly advocate vigilantism, but in our house, we've taken the law into our own hands.

Deception is the key to the Grogan Telemarketing Defense System (TDS).

One night, we were reading in bed when the phone rang. My wife listened for a minute before saying in a heartbreaking voice, "I'm sorry, but no, my husband can't come to the phone. He passed away last night."

She barely got the words out when—click—the telemarketer was on to the next victim. I should have been thrilled, but I don't know. She sounded just a little too gleeful conjuring up my demise. Do I need to be worried?

### The Name Game

Like any military operation, a successful TDS relies on early detection. My wife and I have different last names. Anyone calling for Mrs. Grogan gets a "Sorry, no one here by that name." Click.

.Mangled names are another tip-off. If you don't want me hanging up on you, don't call me "Mr. Gorggins."

Another important weapon is the classic Three H Flanking Maneuver.

Three H was developed by my 87-year-old father, who spent the first 10 years of retirement listening politely to every imaginable come-on before deciding to fight back.

Three H (Hello, Hello, Hang-up) targets the soft underbelly of the telemarketers' primary offensive weapon: the automatic speed dialer.

These rapid-fire dialers are the telemarketing equivalent of howitzers. But they have one fatal flaw: A momentary delay before a live telemarketer can come on the line.

Care to share your technique, Dad?

"You say, 'Hello? Hello?' And, if no one answers, hang up immediately."

Personally, I'm a disciple of Secretary of State Colin Powell's doctrine of overwhelming force. This usually involves letting my 6-year-old daughter answer the phone.

Telemarketer: "Is John Gorggins there?"

Colleen: "Santa brought me a Barbie Bake Oven for Christmas."

And she's off and running for the next 20 minutes, detailing her secrets to cupcake success while steadfastly refusing to hand over the phone.

She wears them down every time.

### Could You Speak Up?

My other secret weapons are my two sons, the aspiring musicians. One is learning trumpet, the other violin.

They like to practice at the same time. In the same room. In different keys. This fools our two dogs into thinking that a cat is being tortured in the immediate vicinity, which sets them to barking ferociously.

Adults who have been in our house during rehearsal ask how we stand it. But I just drink it in, grinning maniacally, one hand on the phone, daring a telemarketer to call.

Go ahead, pal; make my day.

I'll admit, this tactic probably violates the Articles of the Geneva Conventions, but you do what you must.

Of course, blunt honesty works, too.

A couple of months ago, a seriously perky woman called to try to sell me a condo in "New York City's exciting theater district." I cut her off.

"Reality check," I said. "I'm a guy with three kids, two dogs, three pet chickens, and a mortgage that rivals the gross national product of Lithuania. My wife and I consider it a red-letter weekend if we can sneak out alone to the Wawa to buy milk. Then there's the college funds. Do you know—"

Click.

And, gee, I was just getting started.

*April 8, 2003*

## Burning the Flag as an Act of Love

The sun was sinking beneath the horizon, a chill in the air, when I led my children into the backyard to burn the American flag.

It was not an act of anger or rebellion or defiance. Far from it.

Our family's flag was a simple nylon affair, the kind you can pick up for ten bucks at any hardware store. We would haul it out on Memorial Day and the Fourth of July and sometimes just for fun. Truth be told, it had become less patriotic symbol than garden accent. I liked the way it looked hanging off the back deck above the roses and daisies. My wife and I tried to remember to bring it in at night; but for long stretches, it stayed out around the clock, rain or shine.

Over the years, it faded, then frayed, and finally shredded. The last time we had it out—in those dark days after September 11, 2001—a stiff breeze finished it off, ripping it into a series of sad ribbons. I simply rolled the tattered remains around the flagpole and propped it in a corner of the garage.

I knew that was no way to treat the American flag, this proud symbol of freedom and sacrifice; and I promised myself to get around to disposing of it properly. But in a busy suburban life of yard work, home repairs, and soccer matches, it became a low priority.

## What It Stood For

As the weeks turned to months, the old, shredded flag gnawed at me. I began to think about what it really stood for and how many Americans had laid their lives at its feet these 200 years and more.

How many had died on September 11 simply for living beneath its banner. How many continue to fight and die in its name today.

In the face of this new, changed world, there was not much I could do, but I could make right by that old flag.

So on a crisp, clear evening, with a firmament of stars awakening above as if to bear witness, I called my sons, ages 9 and 10, into the garage, and together we gently unclipped our old flag from its pole and folded its shredded remains as best we could into a tight triangle. A former Boy Scout, I had once been quite adept at folding the American flag. But it had been years since I had bothered. It took me a few tries to get it right.

I gave the folded flag to my older boy to carry, and we made our way to the back corner of the yard where the fire circle sits. The boys gathered kindling from beneath the pines. Soon we had a small blaze that we fed with walnut and maple branches until the flames jumped cheerfully into the night.

Seeing the glow, two neighbor boys walked over and joined us. I told them what we were about to do and explained why.

## Moment of Silence

Without prompting, one of the boys asked, "Should we have a moment of silence?" And we all agreed that this would be a good idea. We stood there for a minute or more, the only sound the crackling of the burning hardwood.

Children will sometimes surprise you. This night was one of those times. Again without prompting, one of the boys placed his right hand over his heart and began: "I pledge allegiance to the flag . . ."

And the rest of us joined in. " . . . of the United States of America . . .

"And to the Republic for which it stands . . .

"One nation under God . . .

"Indivisible . . .

"With liberty and justice for all."

I took the flag from my son's arms and nestled it into the burning logs. The flames immediately leapt as the nylon caught fire, and we watched in silence as the Stars and Stripes curled up and disappeared into ashes.

Tattered and worn, this humble flag of ours had graced our home in good times and in very bad times, in joy and in deepest sorrow, in pride and in anguish. It had seen babies arrive and Americans die. Now, however belatedly, it was officially, properly retired.

We stood in a circle for a long time, the boys, normally rambunctious and silly, saying nothing. The orange light of the fire shone on their sweet faces. As much as I tried not to, I found myself thinking about—and hoping against—the war they someday might be called to fight.

Eventually, my younger son spoke. "Dad, will we get another flag?"

"You bet," I said.

*June 27, 2003*

# In Healing,
## Reminder of Life's Final Hurt

As dozens of my colleagues hunkered down with American troops in the Iraqi desert, I was embedded in a life-and-death struggle of an entirely different kind.

My post was a Bucks County nursing home, and the war I witnessed over a six-week period was against that insidious enemy known as age.

Let me tell you, like all wars, this one is hell.

What brought me to the nursing home was not journalistic curiosity but medical necessity. Two herniated disks in my neck sent me in search of a physical therapist. I found a good one who practiced in rented space in the nursing home's basement right beside a small beauty parlor where, each morning, old women caused a traffic jam of wheelchairs as they maneuvered to have their hair set.

Three mornings a week, I arrived for traction and exercise. Several of my fellow patients were just like me, in the words of the physical therapist, "40-something guys who still think they're 20." Middle-age men who stupidly overdid it and hurt themselves.

Yep, that would be me.

But we were the clear minority. Most of the therapist's patients were residents from upstairs. Starting at 8:30 each morning, attendants in bright floral smocks would begin arriving with them. Some came with canes, some with walkers. Most arrived in wheelchairs.

They were stiff and weak and achy—and very old, in the final pages of the long books that are their lives. The physical therapist wasn't pretending to fix them. His job was simply to help them make it through each remaining day a little more comfortably.

Over the weeks, I got to know several of them and the world they inhabit. It is a world most of us breeze past unnoticed as we go about our lives. A world of empty hours and countless days, not unpleasant but without future, where the only checkout is death.

There was Anna, a birdlike woman with a thin wisp of white hair, who rolled in with her arm in a sling from a fall. The therapist and his 24-year-old assistant tried to engage her, get her to do a few light exercises. She would have nothing to do with it.

"Why am I here?" she asked.

"We're going to work on that arm," he said.

"Why can't I hear what you say?"

The therapist let the question slide, but she asked it again, this time more urgently. He knelt before her, his face close to hers, and said loudly but gently, "I think it's age-related, Anna."

There was chubby, cheery Sue, who each morning lay on a low table, struggling to lift her hips a few inches into the air. One day, she smiled sweetly at me and volunteered: "My mother always told me, 'Never get old.'" Then she paused, and the smile slipped from her lips. Somehow it hadn't worked out that way.

Across the room was Doris, hooked to an oxygen tank and dressed improbably in purple high heels. Her mission was to get out of her wheelchair without help. She rocked to build momentum. "One, two, three. Up you go," the assistant coached cheerfully. Doris tried and tried again.

"I just can't do it," she said.

And, saddest of all, there was Violet, who by all appearances had given up. Her job was to tug a rope through a pulley. But she just let the braided cord slip from her lifeless hands.

The therapist admonished: "Come on, Violet. What's going on with you? Show me you still have something in your body to work with."

But Violet was done. Checked out. She sat, gazing blankly ahead.

On my last day, I arrived to find the place nearly empty. All of my elderly friends were missing, and for a brief, sudden second I was filled with sadness. Had their time come? All at once?

But after a few minutes, in they wandered: Doris, still on her oxygen but this time in more sensible shoes; Anna, her bruises turning yellow; always cheerful Sue; rail-thin Ray. And poor Violet.

As they struggled with their routines, wincing and groaning, the young assistant working the muscles in my neck, lowered her lips near my ear, and whispered her confession.

"God, I hope I never get old."

*August 12, 2003*

# Phones Driving Us to Distraction

Not long ago, I was a cell-phone virgin. I didn't own one and didn't want one. I had a phone at work and a phone at home, and that was as in touch with the world as I wanted to be.

My idea of getting wired was gulping a double espresso, not signing my life away to Cingular.

In those B.C. (Before Cell) days, I made sport of ridiculing the self-important chatterbox slaves who were convinced the world would stop—screech to a crashing halt—if they were out of touch for one solitary second. I watched them droning on at restaurants, malls, ballgames, picnics—and wondered what on earth they were finding to jabber about.

Now I'm one of them, a cell-phone convert. And I wonder no more. How I ever got along without one of these things I'll never know. Equipped with my mobile communicator, I feel like Spock on a *Star Trek* episode.

But, like almost everyone else who owns a cell phone, I have a problem. I can't resist using mine—to check voice mail, talk with my editors, return messages—as I hurtle down the expressway in a two-ton steel box at frightening speeds.

As though Philadelphia's crowded roads don't have enough headaches already, they've now been invaded by vast armies of mobile goofus gabbers. To which I say: Reporting for duty, sir!

## That Vision Thing

My favorite soldiers in this assault are the members of the bifocals brigade (of which I am a recent inductee). You see them swerving at you in traffic, with one hand on the steering wheel, the other hand holding their cell phones out at full arm's length as they squint quizzically at the keypad, trying to read the tiny numbers.

We chatty commuters are checking blind spots, passing, and merging into rush hour—all while yammering away about the minutiae of our lives.

If you see us coming, look out, because we won't be looking out for you.

At least when we run each other off the road, we can dial 911 before the wreckage even comes to rest.

Do you think this is what AT&T had in mind when it told us to reach out and touch someone?

A first-ever study of driving habits by the University of North Carolina paints a sobering picture of how distracted motorists have become. The study videotaped drivers in metro Philadelphia and in North Carolina and found that 30 percent talked on cell phones as they drove. The average driver took 13 seconds to dial a cell phone. At 60 miles per hour, that means the car traveled nearly a quarter mile with the driver looking down at the phone. Oh my.

The study found that 40 percent of drivers read or write behind the wheel, usually while stopped. What is this, community college?

An additional 46 percentage groom themselves as they drive, and a whopping 71 percent bring new meaning to the term fast food, eating or drinking as they zoom along. Rule me guilty on that last count. If I add any more selections to my front-seat buffet, I'll need a lunch-wagon license.

## A Close Shave

In my daily commutes, I've seen it all: Women applying makeup; men using electric shavers; couples mashing.

I even know a guy who claims to play guitar while driving. You will note that a guitar requires two hands to play, which leaves approximately no hands to steer with. In his own defense, my friend says he serenades the dashboard only while cruising down lonely stretches of road. Well, why didn't you say so, Elvis?

All this distraction comes at a cost to human safety. As *The Inquirer*'s Marian Uhlman reported last week, it is to blame for roughly a quarter of all car accidents, according to National Highway Traffic Safety Administration estimates.

That's a lot of distraction.

I must confess, since getting my cell phone, I sometimes glance up mid-conversion and have no idea how I got where I am: One second I'm in Baltimore, the next I'm entering Chester. Hey, what happened to Delaware?

So, my fellow crazed commuters, whaddaya say? Shall we try regulating ourselves before the government kindly does it for us?

Here's a place to start: I promise not to call you from the road if you promise not to call me.

*August 25, 2003*

## Hey, Ever Hear of an Ashtray?

Dear Drive-By Smoker:

You don't know me, but I know you.

I was driving behind you in rush hour on the Blue Route a couple of Fridays ago.

You remember the drive, don't you? Traffic was moving at a crawl through a steady rain.

As we inched along in a sea of red brake lights, I had plenty of time to watch you. It wasn't your driving that caught my eye. It was your cigarette.

There was something about the way you held it outside your window, protected from the rain by your cupped hand. There was something about the way you brought it into your new car interior just long enough to draw a quick inhale. Something about the way you cocked your head up to blow the smoke back out the open window and the way you stretched your arm out every half minute to flick the ashes as far as possible from your new Toyota 4Runner.

I could tell you didn't want to stink up your sweet ride. Couldn't blame you; I wouldn't, either.

But your smoking fastidiousness made me uneasy. I had a bad feeling about where that cigarette butt was going to end up.

"He's not," I wondered aloud, "going to toss that thing out the window, is he?"

Cars have ashtrays for a reason. Americans smoke more than 400 billion—yes, billion—cigarettes a year, according to the Department of Agriculture, nearly all of them filtered.

## A Long, Ugly Legacy

Those cigarette filters may look like biodegradable cotton, but they are actually made of stubborn plastic filaments that can take years, even decades, to break down.

Every year, hundreds of millions of these butts are mindlessly flicked out car windows, off patios, over railings, into gardens and, of course, onto beaches where toddlers gravitate to them like candy.

Not only do they become semipermanent additions to the landscape, but the poisons they are designed to trap also slowly leach out and find their way into streams and lakes.

Charming, huh?

So, you see, Drive-By Smoker, I was worried about that butt of yours. One butt may seem like no big deal, but multiply it by 100 million and you have an environmental hazard. What would *you* be? Part of the problem or part of the solution?

I watched as you pulled the smoldering butt back into the car for one long, last drag. The moment of truth had arrived. Would you snuff it out in your car's spotless ashtray? Or would you make the world your ashtray?

I wanted to believe in you. Not all smokers are inconsiderate slobs, right? I've met smokers who are so conscientious they carry small metal canisters in their pockets to hold their butts until they reach a trash can. But they're the exception.

Many smokers, it seems, have convinced themselves that a few billion cigarette butts littering the roadsides of America are no big deal. Each individual butt is so small, it doesn't really count as littering, does it?

I particularly love the smokers who conscientiously use their ashtrays, but then, once full, dump them in public parking lots. Pigs. Total pigs.

### Not a Bad Person

I caught your face in profile a couple of times. You looked like a pretty decent sorta guy who works hard, pays his taxes, maybe coaches Little League. A guy who suffers through rush hour to get home to his family in the suburbs in time for dinner.

You looked like the kind of person who would not consider for a moment tossing a soda can or bag of fast-food debris out your car window.

And yet here you were with a cigarette butt poised in your hand. I watched as you expertly balanced it between your thumb and forefinger and slowly exhaled your final puff.

And then, with a graceful flick, you sent that butt arcing through the dusk and onto the shoulder of the highway, where it sat in a puddle of rainwater.

On behalf of all of us who will live with this little testament to your slovenly thoughtlessness for the next 25 years, I'd like to thank you. On behalf of the fish and birds and animals. On behalf of the plants and soil and water. On behalf of all our children and grandchildren. Thank you for the gift that keeps on giving.

*September 9, 2003*

## Letting Go of the
## One That Got Away

Regrets. Every life has them, some more than others. Lately, I have had just one: the home that got away.

I saw it on my first day of house hunting in Southeastern Pennsylvania, stumbling serendipitously upon it as if led by divine compass. I took a wrong turn and then another, and soon I was hopelessly lost on a stripeless country lane. I followed the lane down a steep hill and through a stand of hardwoods.

And there it was.

Standing close against the trees in a meadow that hadn't been mowed, its limestone walls glowing in the morning sun—an 1840s farmhouse. A glorious, lovely farmhouse with deep windowsills, a slate roof, and a porch from which you could imagine the original owners waving farewell as their sons trudged off to defend the Union.

It sat on five rolling acres with a spring and a view. And there was a for-sale sign out front. Gulp!

This was the place my wife and I had dreamed of. The garden could go here, the chicken coop there. Best of all, a tiny stone cottage, which I later learned was the original homestead, still stood on the edge of the property—a writing studio waiting to happen.

I was soon back with my wife and a real estate agent. She pushed open the front door, and our hearts sank.

**The Money Pit**

Walls were caved in. Floors scarred. Ceilings buckled. Loose wiring hung from the rafters. The kitchen was missing in action. A hot plate and dirty dishes on the toilet told us where the cooking now was done.

Suddenly I knew why the house was in our price range. Everywhere we looked we saw work—and bills. The plumbing, the wiring, the plaster, the chimney, the heating, the cellar all required overhauls. Tens of thousands of dollars were needed just to make it habitable, and tens of thousands more—and hundreds of hours of our time—if it were ever to reclaim its charm.

And still, after a brief ashen silence, my wife and I began plotting.

"This wall could come out," I said.

"The kitchen could go here," she said.

Our agent stood quietly. She had seen it all before. The young couples with big dreams and the way these stone seductresses lured them in, chewed them up, and spat them out, broke and broken.

Finally, she frowned and said: "You have three young children and a new job. In good conscience, I cannot let you buy this place." She knew the score. We could barely afford the asking price, let alone the needed renovations. And I wasn't exactly Bob Vila.

Still, we dithered. We agonized. We wrote up a five-year work plan. In the end, we followed our agent's advice and bought a sensible, suburban two-story with maintenance-free vinyl siding and a new furnace.

And lived happily ever after. Well, almost. It was just our luck that we became close friends with the people next door to the old farmhouse. Every time we visited, we were reminded of our choice. For months, the house stood empty, and we felt only relief. We congratulated ourselves for not stumbling into that sorry quagmire.

### A Vision Realized

But then a young couple bought the place and began doing everything we had dreamed of doing. They mowed down the weeds, raised a barn, dug a pond, erected a split-rail fence.

Then one day at dinner at our friends', we met them. And they invited us over to see the inside. We could not believe it was the same house. Walls had been moved, the plaster repaired and painted, the plank floors refinished, a new kitchen installed.

We gushed about the wonderful job they had done. But I saw it behind my wife's smile, and she saw it behind mine. Inside, we were aching.

It was our house just as we had imagined it. But it wasn't ours. It was the one we let get away. Regrets.

I wanted to begrudge this couple their trophy. Quite honestly, I wanted to hate them. But they were much too nice for that. I had to admit they possessed what I did not: the energy, skill, creativity and, most important, faith in their vision to pull it off.

Yes, and the money, too.

Where I saw nothing but heartache, they saw limitless potential.

They deserve their trophy manor. And I'm learning to love my consolation prize, vinyl siding and all.

*October 7, 2003*

## Haunting Glimpse at a Stranger's Life

A month has passed, and still she haunts me.

From vastly different worlds, we came briefly together— a middle-aged, white man from the suburbs and a young black woman from the projects.

We never even said our names.

I was driving into the faded Western Pennsylvania steel city of Johnstown on assignment—and was lost.

I exited the expressway to ask directions and found myself amid several low-slung brown buildings—a subsidized housing project. Young men stood about in groups, killing time. On a street corner near them, a wisp of a girl stood alone.

She wore her hair in a short, stubby ponytail, and the wire-framed glasses perched on her nose gave her the look of a schoolgirl. I rolled down my window and asked how to get downtown.

She began to try to direct me, and then she stopped and looked at the sky as if trying to solve a riddle.

"You know what?" she said. "I've been standing here for an hour waiting for the bus, and if I don't get downtown in the next half hour, I'm sunk."

"Can I have a ride?"

Could she have a ride? In the seconds that ticked by before I answered, I thought of a hundred reasons why, no, she could not.

We were strangers. She didn't know if she could trust me. I didn't know if I could trust her. She was just a kid. In 2003, young women do not get into cars with strange men, do they? And men of honorable intent don't allow them to, do they?

## The Whiff of Impropriety

And there was the appearance. Older guy pulls up alongside much younger woman on street corner; she leans in, then gets in. I could just see myself explaining it to the vice detail waiting around the corner.

Everything said no. And yet something about this young woman told me she really needed this ride. "I could show you the way," she offered.

I hesitated one last moment, then blurted out, "Sure. Hop in."

Before I could clear the junk off the front passenger seat, she slid into the backseat. And I knew from her expression that this was a defensive move—the farthest seat from my reach.

"Late for work?" I asked as we drove off through the stares of the idle young men. But there was no job.

She was 20 years old and the single mother of a 16-month-old daughter. She needed to get to the courthouse before it closed, she said, or else the baby's father would be going to jail for failing to pay child support.

"I need to tell them he's a good man," she said. "He's a good dad."

A good dad leaves her to raise this child alone? She said putting him in jail would solve nothing.

She told me she had grown up in Erie as a ward of the state, being bounced from one foster home to the next. The day she turned 18 was the day she struck out on her own with dreams of building a better life.

## Flight to Nowhere

"Why Johnstown?" I asked.

She shrugged. "Because it wasn't Erie," she answered.

Soon she was pregnant. By 19, she was a mother, alone no more but with no way to support herself and her child except for government assistance. How differently life might have turned out for her, I wondered, had she been dealt the basic hand every child deserves: a stable home and loving parents.

What if someone had believed in her worth and let her know it? What might she be now?

A college student? An apprentice in a trade? A woman on the first rung of her career? Perhaps she would be something other than on public assistance facing an uphill battle to avoid repeating for her daughter the same poverty and dependency she herself was born into.

I pulled in front of the courthouse, and she opened the car door.

"Thanks for the ride," she said.

As much as you can like someone after 20 minutes, I liked her. I wanted to tell her that it was not too late to reach for her dreams. She was 20 years old with her whole life ahead of her. She could still make something better of it. I wanted to tell her she owed it to her daughter to try.

What I said instead was. "Good luck." And I meant it.

She smiled, then loped across the street and through the big courthouse doors with nine minutes to spare.

*January 20, 2004*

## Let No Chip Put This Vow Asunder

I waited until the kids were on the school bus before I confronted my wife by the coffeemaker and said: "Honey, I have a confession to make."

She looked at me with that nervous grin she gets when bracing for the worst.

"I cheated," I said. "I'm sorry."

"I can't believe this," she said.

It was true. I had violated our shared vow of carbohydrate celibacy and low-fat fidelity. I had strayed from our joint diet—straight into the crunchy embrace of a bag of Doritos. I wish I could say I didn't enjoy it, but I did. Each bite was pure bliss.

Believe me, I'm not proud of myself.

As my wife pointed out, we had a deal, struck during a calorie-crazed vacation to Disney World over Christmas. "This is it," I said as we polished off chocolate-covered ice cream bars outside Space Mountain. "When we get home, we're going on a diet."

My cheapskate gene had finally trumped my chowhound gene. I either had to drop 10 pounds and a couple of inches or replace my wardrobe.

Jenny is lanky by design. But she, too, has noticed that one of the many charming aspects of rounding the halfway point to 90—along with those stylish Grandpa Walton bifocals and an utter inability to stay awake through the 11 o'clock news—is that calories no longer burn themselves into oblivion as they once did.

### Till Chips Do We Part

"I'm in," she said. And right then we exchanged our vows. We would support and encourage each other, on good weigh-in days and bad, in fullness and in hunger, through cake cravings and linguine lusts.

Many of our friends were on low-carbohydrate diets, and, frankly, it didn't sound all that tough. You still got to eat all the good stuff like steak and ham. All you were cutting out were the things that went around them—the rice and pasta and breads and sweets. How hard could that be?

New Year's Day came, and we launched our diet by dropping in on our friends Mike and Patti for an impromptu pizza-and-beer party. "Here's to our new low-carb diet!" I toasted.

The next day, we got another invitation for pizza and beer. "Tomorrow, we start for sure." I vowed. And we did.

Life knows no joy like opening the day with runny eggs without toast washed down with unsweetened coffee. My children taunted me by gnawing on huge, doughy bagels.

By dinner (a chicken breast with salad), I was so crazed for carbs I nearly tackled my son as he carried a bowl of macaroni to the table. That night I dreamed of bread and butter.

By Day 3, I was fantasizing about being locked overnight in a bakery. On Day 7, I looked out the window and saw plates of steaming rigatoni floating by. On Day 9, I said to Jenny: "My wardrobe needs updating, anyway."

And on Day 10, I spotted the Doritos.

### Surrendering to Desire

The bag lay on top of the refrigerator, wantonly open, barely folded over. O, be still my low-carb cheatin' heart!

I stepped closer. The bag's siren call filled my ears, seeming to say: "You know you want me." I knew I did. My arm, of its own volition, reached up.

"Look away from the chips!" my dieting partner barked. Busted.

But it was only a matter of time. In my heart, I had already strayed. For the next couple of days I searched for excuses to walk past the refrigerator, shooting furtive glances up at the little home-wrecker.

Jenny and I had each lost a few pounds. The diet was working. But at what cost? Was a life without bread and pie and chips and beer—did I mention no beer?—worth living?

And so, I did it. Late that night, when everyone was asleep, I lit into the bag. Just one chip, I promised. Then it was two. Then three. Soon I lost count.

The next day, a few hours after my confession, my wife called me at work. "I just ate popcorn," she said. "With butter."

"Oh, that is so like a woman," I seethed. "One little lapse on your husband's part and you're dragging home Orville Redenbacher."

Eventually, we worked things out. The joint diet is holding—by a thread. It may take counseling, but I think we're going to get through this.

And you know what? Our marriage will be stronger for it. Assuming, of course, a warm loaf of bread doesn't show up at the door anytime soon.

# He Helps Iraq's Children
# and America's Cause

Until a little more than a year ago, Thomas Murt was just another suburban dad.

He coached youth sports for his three children's teams and taught catechism at St. David's Catholic Church in Willow Grove.

He was an Upper Moreland Township commissioner and made his living as an academic adviser at Pennsylvania State University's Abington campus. Life was comfortable.

Then on January 24, 2003, the fax machine in his office rattled out a slip of paper that would change everything.

Murt's Army Reserve unit was being sent to Iraq. Less than 24 hours later, he was on a plane to Fort Drum, New York, and within weeks found himself on the ground in Saddam Hussein's volatile hometown of Tikrit. "He was gone before we really had a chance to say goodbye," his wife, Maria, said.

It was there in the desert sands that this man's ordinary life took a turn for the extraordinary. On his own, he has informally adopted hundreds of impoverished Iraqi children—and in so doing he is helping the United States win its biggest battle of all, the battle for the trust of the Iraqi people.

Staff Sargent Murt, 43, who resigned his elected Upper Moreland post when he was deployed, was assigned to serve as a bodyguard and driver for his company commander. He also provided security for civil-affairs missions into the countryside, which included the rebuilding of local schools.

The frequent forays into remote villages gave him an up-close look at what life was like for thousands of ordinary Iraqis, nearly all of them living in abject poverty. The children especially moved him. Most had no schoolbooks or pencils, nor even a sweater or single pair of socks to see them through the cold winter.

Murt has always had a soft spot for children in need. His wife, who has been managing the family home for more than a year now as a single parent, remembers the couple's 1989 honeymoon to Grenada. Without telling her, Murt brought along two large suitcases filled with clothing and toys for children at a local orphanage.

"It's just always been part of him," she said.

Now in Iraq, Murt saw a whole new level of need. And he got an idea. His coworkers and neighbors had been sending him boxes of toiletries and gifts to share with his fellow soldiers.

He appreciated the outpouring but felt the generosity could be better directed. So he sent e-mails to everyone he knew, with photos of the Iraqi children he had befriended, asking them instead to send old clothing, toys, costume jewelry, and school supplies.

"Many of the things we take for granted in the U.S. are great luxuries here," he wrote.

From around Upper Moreland and Willow Grove and Hatboro, the community responded, and boxes of donated goods began to roll in. Dozens of boxes, shipped by domestic mail to Fort Drum, then aboard military transport planes to Iraq, all addressed to Murt, "He was well known at the [base] mail room," his wife said.

His coworkers at Penn State Abington sent 35 boxes. Boy Scout Troop 336 in Willow Grove collected 935 pounds of school supplies. At St. David's, Sister Rita, the principal, put out the call for children to scour their toy chests.

Pete's Barber Shop in Hatboro got in on the act. So did many neighbors. Annie Gleave, who works at the Hatboro post office and took a lead in organizing donations, said Murt's photos of shoeless Iraqi children touched her. "It's made me see what's really important in life," she said.

And Murt said the community's outpouring, in turn, has touched the Iraqi children and their families. Many now consider the Americans their friends.

"By working with the children and villagers, we have a golden opportunity to teach them that we are not their enemy," wrote Murt, who hopes to be home in the next six to eight weeks and asks that no more donations be sent.

And isn't that where victory lies? One soldier, one community winning over a country one child at a time.

Said Upper Moreland resident Kathy Rusch, who was involved in the donation drive: "With Tom, this is not an unusual thing. This is how he lives his life. He is just one of those people who gives a damn."

## TV Weather Is a Flurry of Hysteria

As I watched from my kitchen window yesterday morning as a few snowflakes drifted down, melting as they touched the pavement, a terrifying chill ran through me.

Not another one, I thought. Not another flashback to the winter that will live in infamy. No, it wasn't the season's weather that had me unwound. The weather was just fine, actually on the wimpy side for Pennsylvania.

It was the television news coverage of the weather that left me quaking. This was the year of the hysterical "We all could die!" winter-storm alert.

No matter how modest the dusting outside, you could turn on any of the local television stations and hear something that went like this:

(Dramatic music plays; a video montage shows howling blizzard conditions, the likes of which have not been seen in this region for years.)

We interrupt this program for a special storm advisory.

Anchor Brent Blowdried: Well, folks, this is what all of us have been dreading. What just might be the storm of the century may be heading our way, bringing with it the possibility of death, destruction, mayhem, and indescribable heartbreak.

Co-anchor Brenda Bigteeth: That's right, Brent. This could be one for the record books. Our team coverage begins right now at the base of the Walt Whitman Bridge where reporter Bunny Snowsuit is standing by. Bunny, what can you tell us?

Snowsuit: We now have confirmed sightings of at least seven—I repeat, seven—snowflakes sticking to the bridge behind me. And we understand they're whoppers! If this keeps up, commuters could have one hellish drive ahead of them in the morning. Back to you, Brent and Brenda.

Blowdried: Chilling stuff, Bunny. It sounds like the best bet is for folks to just stay home and stay tuned right here to the Storm Advisory Center.

Snowsuit: That's right, Brent. Unless you absolutely must venture out, we're urging everyone to stay off the roads— and stay glued to this station for the latest developments.

Bigteeth: Good advice, Bunny. And now to give a historical perspective on just how tragic severe winter storms can be for those who venture out, national correspondent Alexa Alarmista has prepared this report.

Alarmista: Brenda, I'm standing here at the Donner Pass, where in 1846 dozens of westbound commuters met slow, agonizing deaths in a snow-choked mountain pass not unlike our own Schuylkill Expressway.

Bigteeth: And do I understand some actually resorted to cannibalism?

Alarmista: Sadly, that's true, Brenda. Another good reason to stay home and stay glued to our live coverage. I'm Alexa Alarmista, reporting live from the Donner Pass.

Blowdried: Well, we certainly don't want a repeat of that here in Greater Philadelphia. Thank you, Alexa, and stay safe out there.

Bigteeth: Alexa will be back at 11 with her next install-
ment: "Avalanches—What You Need to Know."

Blowdried: Our team coverage continues with con-
sumer reporter Dennis Dumbdown, who is standing by
live at the Sparkle Car Wash in Bucks County with a
helpful snow-safety tip.

Dumbdown: With me here is Langhorne resident
Shirley Yoojest who has survived years of winter storms
by using her wits. Shirley is going to demonstrate for us a
snow-survival technique that could save your life.

Yoojest (tapping foot against side of car): Well, basically, I
always make a point to knock the snow off my boots before I get in my car. Some people wait until they're already
in their car.

Dumbdown: And by then it could be too late! That
harmless boot snow could be transformed in a heartbeat
into a potential killer: brake-pedal black ice!

Blowdried: Fascinating stuff. We now turn to meteorol-
ogist Alfie "Mudpuddle" Dorkman with the latest Hype-
U-Weather Forecast.

Dorkman: Clouds, clouds everywhere, people. Don't be
lulled into complacency by the dry pavement. By morning, all bets could be off.

Bigteeth: Mudpuddle, am I hearing you say that tomorrow would be an excellent day to call in sick and spend
the day right here with us at the Hype-U-Weather Storm
Advisory Center?

Dorkman: Bingo, Brenda. And now if you'll excuse me,
I need to go count ratings—er, I mean snowflakes.

# Ordinary People
# Vowing to Marry

In many ways, they are a typical suburban couple.

They spend their weekends remodeling their tidy three-bedroom house, which sits on a quiet street in the Main Line community of Strafford. They enjoy gardening and cooking and spoiling their dog, Cybil.

They both come from large, traditional Catholic families, and they dote on their 17 nieces and nephews.

Now in their early 50s, they prefer quiet nights at home to going out on the town. They pay their taxes on time, look in on sick neighbors, and vote each election.

They are ordinary in all ways but one: Tim Dineen and Victor Martorano, a couple for nine years, are homosexuals. And that puts them squarely in the middle of the national debate on same-sex marriage.

They are not the ones protesting on courthouse steps or trying to force change by seeking marriage licenses where they know none will be issued. As the debate rages, they have written letters to newspapers, but otherwise go quietly about their suburban lives. It was for this reason— their very ordinariness—that I sought them out last week. I wanted to see for myself just how different from the heterosexual majority a gay couple in a long-term relationship is.

## Marriage of the Minds

They give me a tour of their house and show off improvements they have made—new tile, enlarged kitchen, hardwood floors. On the table is a vase of pussy willows brought in from the garden. Outside, a pile of rain gutters sits in the yard, next weekend's project.

In their own minds, Dineen, a demonstration chef at a Trader Joe's market in nearby Wayne, and Martorano, who works in the travel industry, already are married. On their first Christmas together, they privately exchanged gold bands that have remained on their left ring fingers ever since. Still, says Dineen, "we will get married the day we legally can do it."

Some of the motivation is practical. If one is incapacitated, the other right now would need a written power of attorney to make medical decisions—a precaution they already have taken. And as Dineen pointed out over a cup of coffee, "If Victor died tomorrow, I would have to pay inheritance tax on his half of our house."

Adds Martorano: "The law does not recognize me as his next of kin, and that is wrong. It's just wrong."

But more important to the couple is what marriage stands for—a public acknowledgement of a couple's love and lifelong commitment. "Marriage is a stabilizing force in society," Dineen says, "and we want to be part of that stabilization."

After all, they consider themselves solid members of the community. And so do their neighbors. As Peg Schwartz, 73 and a registered Republican, told me later: "I can't say enough about them. They really could not be better neighbors. They are delightful. They're just nice, kind, caring people, and that's what you want in a neighbor." Having them next door has softened her position on gay marriage, she said. "If that makes them happy, then that's all that counts."

## Battling Stereotypes

And yet, for now at least, Dineen and Martorano will remain the one couple on their street for whom the civil contract of marriage is not an option. Until that day comes, the two men believe stereotypes and prejudice will continue.

"Gay people have a reputation for being extremely promiscuous," says Dineen, whose full beard and wireframed glasses give him a professorial air. "Well, not all gay people are."

Some of them lead their lives not much differently from the straight people on their streets, sharing the same worries and joys and dreams. And that brings Dineen to his main point.

"If we were married tomorrow, the only thing that would be different would be the piece of paper that grants us our rights and responsibilities. Nothing else would change. We would still be here just as we are today, putting new gutters on the house, going to work, grocery shopping, taking the dog to the vet."

He adds: "I think that's what so many people fail to realize. We're here already. We're a couple already. For all intents and purposes, we are married. We just lack the legalities."

## Sounds of Spring
## Roar in the Burbs

Outside my window, it looked like the Indianapolis 500—a sure sign that spring once again had returned to the suburbs.

From all directions came the roar of engines, the smell of exhaust, and the violent gnashing of blades.

Yes, folks, after a long peaceful winter, that darling of the suburban experience is back in force once again: grass-cutting season.

And last weekend, with its July-worthy temperatures, marked the unofficial but widely observed kickoff—the ceremonial first cut. Out where I live, this is no small deal.

I knew the big day had finally arrived when I awoke Saturday to the growl of Toros and John Deeres. Homeowners, start your engines!

Outside, up and down my street, I saw the same thing: grown men (and a few women) perched on brightly colored riding mowers, zipping gleefully across the landscape at full throttle. Grass clippings flew, and the air held that sweet perfume of gasoline mixed with crushed chlorophyll.

Honestly, my neighbors looked ridiculous out there, perched on their low-riding mowing machines, knees up to their chests like so many Shriners on go-carts.

My reaction was swift and predictable: "Dang! I've got to get out there!"

## Conformity Calls

Here it was mid-April, and my tractor was still in the corner of the garage pinned beneath a pile of coiled hoses and folded lawn chairs. Late again. If I didn't want to get banned from the next neighborhood potluck, I knew I had better bring my shaggy lawn into compliance pronto.

So I spent my weekend—a gorgeous weekend, perfect for hiking or bicycling or simply snoozing in a hammock—on my knees in the garage, sharpening blades, tightening belts, and changing oil. And then with a roar and a cloud of blue smoke, I, too, was off to the races.

My lawnless friends from the city just don't get it, this communal grass fanaticism. I'm hard-pressed to explain it myself, even as I spend two hours a week every week, April through October, embracing it.

It's totally crazy. And totally costly.

There is the price of the machines themselves, which can exceed that of a nice used automobile. There are the repairs and maintenance, the gasoline and fertilizer and pesticides. There are the hours—thousands of them each season in my subdivision alone—that could be spent doing better things. There are the costs to the environment, both from emissions and those millions of tiny gas spills.

And for what? A bumper crop that we neither eat nor sell nor even feed to our pets. With the fervor in which we grow this stuff, you would think we were all goat herders.

We fertilize it so it will grow like crazy, then we cut like crazy just to keep up. That leaves piles of clippings, which we rake and bag beneath the hot sun. And what do we do with this harvest? We place it on the curb and pay someone to haul it away.

## Who's Using Whom?

It all makes you wonder who is actually calling the shots. Are we humans exploiting Kentucky bluegrass and fescue to tame our environment and improve our lives? Or are the grasses exploiting us to spread their dominion across the countryside? Think about it. When was the last time a blade of grass spent its hard-earned paycheck keeping you groomed?

A few hardy souls are fighting back. One couple I know replaced their sod with a native wildflower meadow that required no cutting, no fertilizers, no pesticides. You want to know how well the new look was embraced in their community? They were reported for creating a public nuisance.

I fight back in my own modest way, which is to say I follow the lazy man's guide to lawn care. It's strictly tough love: no fertilizers, no chemicals, no raking, no bagging. I cut it once a week, not a day more frequently.

Predictably, my lawn is a veritable United Nations of weeds. But they all get along reasonably well, and from a passing car at a certain speed, the overall effect keeps me just this side of banishment from the neighborhood association. The difference between the über suburban lawn and my own ragtag wannabe, I have found, comes down to this: 25 miles per hour.

## Earth Versus the Mall People

A government spy satellite roaming the Milky Way in search of extraterrestrial life has picked up a transmission coming from an unknown planet.

Buzzzzzzzz. Schplunkt!

"Commander, I have just returned from my reconnaissance trip to the planet Earth."

"Ah, very good, Cygot. And what did you find there?"

"It is a strange and incomprehensible place. I landed in a confederacy of united but deeply divided states, some red, some blue. There was a place called Joisey, where the people speak a monosyllabic guttural dialect. And a place named Philly where the local language is even harder to decipher. But the oddest findings came in the countryside, in a vast sprawling kingdom called Suburbia."

"What did you see in this Suburbia?"

"I saw heavily armed men dress in orange and headed out into the woods where they blasted away at anything that moved, sometimes hitting each other, sometimes hitting four-legged life forms. And yet at the end of each day they returned to eat an odd energy roll known as 'cheesesteak.'"

"Strange indeed."

"And that's just the beginning, commander. I arrived on a day called Thanksgiving, a tribal holiday to count blessings."

"And how do they mark this sacred day?"

"By eating vast quantities of food, sir. Some even un-button their pants."

"And then what do they do with all this energy they have consumed?"

"They sleep, sir."

## A Predawn Sojourn

"A sort of hibernation?"

"Not exactly. The feast appears to be the start of a vast national marathon they call 'Just 29 Shopping Days to Christmas.' Within hours they are up again, and they head off in darkness to giant edifices surrounded by acres of a gray stonelike surface."

"Their sacred temples, no doubt."

"Yes, and they call these temples all the same name: Mall. The worshippers wait for hours to get inside the doors."

"And what do they do once inside?"

"They use small plastic cards to spend riches they do not have for goods they do not need."

"Goods they do not need?"

"Such as clear stones the slave class digs from the earth."

"They pay vast sums for mere stones?"

"The males hand them to the females who then agree to bear their progeny."

"A fertility rite! And what else?"

"The females wear ceremonial gold and buy expensive pouches to hold their plastic cards. They buy paint for their faces and many pairs of leather coverings for their feet."

"Why many pairs when they have but one pair of feet?"

"Inexplicable, commander, but their closets overflow with them. And the men fill their garages with the lumbering personal transporters known as SUVs, which suck finite fossil fuels from the ground and force the nations to battle each other."

## Zombie Nation

"And who commands them to buy these useless things?"

"The orders come from the Great Persuaders, who rule from a place called Madison Avenue. They decide what the masses must buy and send messages through the electronic tubes in every dwelling, telling the people they are nothing without these items."

"And the people fall for this?"

"No questions asked, sir. Especially during the Christmas 29-day marathon."

"And how is this race won?"

"It seems the household with the most items on Christmas Day is the winner."

"And how do they celebrate?"

"I am told they will awaken before dawn the day after and return to the mall temples, where they exchange the many things they acquired during the marathon for yet more possessions."

"And they do this to celebrate this day they call Christmas?"

"They call it a religious holiday."

"And what is this day? Surely, it must stand for more than that which the plastic card can obtain."

"It once did, I am told, commander. But the people became blinded at the mall temples, and the original meaning appears to have been lost long ago."

"Cygot, your excellent surveillance disturbs me greatly. Now to the decontamination unit before the Earthling consumption disease gets loose."

*December 13, 2004*

## Tow-Truck Driver
## Became Her Angel

What had begun as just another family reunion at Philadelphia International Airport escalated quickly into a life-or-death race against the clock.

Mary Helene Wagner, 78, had just arrived at the airport at dusk November 9 after an uneventful flight from her home in Oakland, California. Waiting to greet her at the gate were her sister, Katherine "Kitti" Colucci, 65, and Kitti's husband, Richard, of Little Egg Harbor, near Atlantic City.

The threesome chatted as they loaded Wagner's bags into the Coluccis' car in the parking garage.

That's when it happened.

"Kitti suddenly cried out in pain and put her hands to her forehead," Wagner said. She moaned about an excruciating headache and began to vomit.

"She started to scream, 'My head, my head,'" Colucci's husband added.

"I knew we had to move," the older sister said. "I said to Richard, 'We have to get to an emergency room.'"

But where, and how? None of them were familiar with Philadelphia, and there was no one in sight to ask. They drove out of the garage and asked the parking attendant for directions, but because of a language barrier, they could not understand what he was trying to tell them.

They headed off into the darkness, knowing each lost minute could make a terrible difference. "I was looking around; I didn't know the area at all. I realized we were in trouble," Richard Colucci said.

### A Brief Touch

He pulled into an Exxon station and frantically asked a customer for directions, but again without luck. His wife was again vomiting out of the car, cradling her head.

That's when Wagner spotted the least likely of guardian angels—a member of that profession area motorists love to hate: a Greater Philly tow-truck driver. He was filling the gas tank on his big lime-green wrecker, and Wagner figured he must know the way to the nearest hospital.

"I approached him for help. He was trying to tell me what to do, but I think he could see the look on my face," she said. "He reached out and touched me, put his hand on my shoulder and said, 'Follow me.'"

Yellow emergency lights flashing, the driver led them through rush-hour traffic, winding his way across the city until he pulled up at the emergency-room doors of the Hospital of the University of Pennsylvania. The driver hesitated just long enough to make sure the Coluccis reached the curb.

"He tooted his horn, turned off his [emergency] lights, and just drove away," Wagner said. "We never saw the side of the truck, the name or anything."

All she knew of the mystery man was his first name, James.

Only after they were inside did they fully realize just what a crucial role the stranger had played in the emergency. Not only had he quickly led Kitti Colucci, who had suffered a triple ruptured brain aneurysm, to a hospital, he led her to the right hospital.

As one of the nation's top medical centers, HUP had a team of neurologists on duty to begin immediate aid when the Coluccis walked in.

## An Angel in Disguise?

Doctors confirmed that in such a case, every second counted. Without the tow-truck driver's intervention, Richard Colucci said, "most likely Kitti would have died. We'll never know for sure."

More than a month later, she remains hospitalized and faces long rehabilitation. But she is alive, and her husband and sister won't forget the kind stranger.

"I want him to know we are very grateful," Wagner said. "I hate to think about what would have happened had we [stopped at the gas station] and James hadn't been there."

Richard Colucci believes it was more than coincidence. "I personally feel that somebody upstairs was looking out for us," he said. "This fellow was there for a purpose."

He wished he could find the driver.

"I would embrace him if I could. I would thank him, and I would tell him that he was an angel," Colucci said.

"That might sound corny, but I really mean it. You have to understand, we were looking at life and death."

Colucci might get his chance.

Tomorrow, I will introduce you to the mystery Good Samaritan, and tell you how I located him.

*December 14, 2004*

## James Pratt
### *A Knight in a Lime-Green Tow Truck*

The Good Samaritan in the lime-green tow truck is a mystery no more.

His name is James Pratt, and he is a 30-year-old single dad who graduated from Germantown High School, Class of '91, and served in the army in Germany before earning a discharge because of a bad back. He now lives in Conshohocken with his daughter. "She turns 5 on Christmas Day," he said.

Pratt makes his living patrolling a stretch of I-95 under contract with the Pennsylvania Department of Transportation, swooping in to help stranded motorists and remove disabled vehicles to keep traffic moving.

He was just ending his shift on the evening of November 9 when he pulled into the Airport Exxon station at Philadelphia International Airport to refuel.

That's when his life intersected with the lives of Mary Helene Wagner, 78, of Oakland, California; Wagner's sister, Kitti Colucci, 65, of Little Egg Harbor, New Jersey; and Kitti's husband, Richard.

As I described yesterday, the Coluccis had just picked up Wagner from Philadelphia International Airport when Kitti Colucci was struck without warning by a searing, violent headache and vomiting, the result, she would later learn, of a triple ruptured brain aneurysm. The three were lost and in desperate need of a hospital.

Wagner ran up to the tow-truck driver, and he began to give her directions. But two things became immediately clear to Pratt: Every second was of the essence, and the frantic travelers were not going to be able to find the hospital on their own.

"Follow me," he told her and then, yellow lights flashing, led the family through rush-hour traffic to the Hospital of the University of Pennsylvania where more than one month later Kitti Colucci continues to recover.

The Coluccis and Wagner were grateful to the tow-truck driver who led them to the front doors of the hospital, but they had no way of telling him so. He had vanished without giving them anything but his first name. And so Wagner called me.

Based on the little she knew—a lime-green truck and an Exxon station near the terminal—I was able to find Pratt through his boss, Kevin Bowe, a Conshohocken-based tow operator who runs Airport Exxon and has the PennDot Expressway Safety Service Patrol contract.

"I'm not really surprised," Bowe said when told of his employee's actions to help the stricken woman. "He's a good guy."

Pratt downplayed what he had done. He was about to drive back to Conshohocken anyway, he said, and the hospital was not that big a detour.

"I just told them to follow my lights," he recalled. "I got them to the front door of the hospital and kept going. I never heard anything after the fact."

When I told him that Richard Colucci had credited his good deed with saving his wife's life, Pratt hesitated a moment before saying, "That's a pleasant plus. It's a beautiful thing to know." He had no idea just how significant his small act of kindness was to these desperate strangers who had stumbled upon him.

As a tow-truck driver, he said, he is either loved or hated. Loved by those who are stranded and he rescues; hated by those who are parked illegally and he tows. "You learn to take the good with the bad," he said.

Helping the Coluccis in their moment of need, he added, was one of the good moments that "helps your job balance itself out."

And it served as a reminder to us all that even in a city as proudly gruff as Philadelphia, in an age when people too often shrug off getting involved, at a time when too many ask, "What's in it for me?" there are still those knights among us who don't hesitate to come to the rescue of perfect strangers simply because it is the right and decent thing to do.

"It shows that there still are good people in this world," a grateful Richard Colucci said.

Responded Pratt as he headed to his next call: "Hey, it's no problem. That's what I do. That's why I'm out here."

*February 1, 2005*

## Zero Tolerance Running Amok

Today's question: How can we adults expect our children to respect us and our decisions when so often we act like total blockheads?

How can we ask them to accept our edicts without question when too often those edicts, however well-intentioned, are so wildly misguided?

Take zero-tolerance policies in our schools. They are in place for a reason. Weapons and drugs have no place in schools. But the words zero and tolerance, when combined, add up to one scary concept: blind enforcement with no room for common sense.

And when that happens, what are we left with? Injustice. And kids who lose faith and grow jaded. No wonder they look at us like we were just beamed down from Planet Clueless.

Exhibit A: The case of the crampy honors student.

As reported by Stephanie L. Arnold in Saturday's *Inquirer*, a senior on the honor roll at Haverford High

School had the temerity to take an over-the-counter pain medication—a generic version of Aleve—for menstrual cramps without first clearing it with the school nurse.

Mind you, she is 18, old enough to fight and die in Iraq. Mind you, she was not misusing the pain medicine. Mind you, she made no attempt to hide her behavior. In fact, she was busted after she went to the nurse and reported that her cramping continued, despite the pill she took.

## A World Without Grays

Does this sound like a crazed drug abuser to you? In the black-and-white world of zero tolerance, the question is moot. She violated the school's drug policy, which bans students from, among other things, taking medication without permission. And she was suspended, if only for part of one day, before she apologized and was allowed back in school.

The girl's mother about nailed it when she likened the policy to "throwing a hand grenade on an anthill."

Unfortunately, the problem is not isolated, which leads to Exhibit B: The case of the handcuffed 10-year-old.

Porsche Brown, a fourth grader at Holme Elementary School in Northeast Philadelphia, was suspended after an 8-inch pair of scissors was found in her book bag. But the saga did not end there. Police arrived, handcuffed the pint-size fugitive, and carted her down to the local precinct house in the back of a police wagon.

Geez, I'd hate to see what they would have done had she been packing a stapler and Elmer's glue.

It's more than a little ridiculous. It's plain dumb. Everyone agrees the child meant no harm in bringing the scissors to school. Yet, at the time, the police policy was to cuff all weapons suspects, regardless of age. And so a child was treated like a criminal.

Schools chief Paul Vallas and city Police Commissioner Sylvester Johnson later apologized to the girl's mother, admitting the principal and cops overreacted. Ya think?

### A Syrup-Crusted Blade

And, finally, consider Exhibit C: The case of the sticky eating utensil.

This one involves yet another honors student, Peter DeWitt, a senior at Great Valley High School in Chester County. DeWitt's car was singled out for a drug search in the school's parking lot in September. No drugs were found, but authorities did spot a small penknife and a steak knife.

DeWitt explained that he used the penknife to tinker with his car stereo. The steak knife had been used by his sister, who ate a plate of waffles in the car on the way to school with him. The parents—who, by supplying the waffles, I suppose were accessories to the crime—confirmed his story.

The alleged weapons never even left the confines of the locked car. Harmless enough, you say? Sorry, no room for reason. Under zero tolerance, DeWitt faced possible expulsion until cooler heads prevailed three days into his suspension.

In each of these cases lurks a glimmer of justification. Children can and do harm themselves by improperly taking medications. Children can and do use something as innocuous as scissors or a utensil to harm others.

There should be no room in schools for harmful behavior of any type. But there should be room for common sense, discretion, and intelligence.

If we want our kids to respect authority, we owe them that much.

*March 14, 2005*

## It's Unhealthy, But It Is Legal

When I was 10, my best friend and I rode our bikes to the local bowling alley, slipped 35 cents into the vending machine, and bought our first pack of cigarettes.

In the woods nearby, we lit up—and promptly turned green. I decided then and there that if this was what it took to be cool, I'd gladly go through life as a dweeb.

To this day, I have little tolerance for cigarette smoke and even less for those inconsiderate slobs who think it is their God-given right to light up anytime, anyplace—and then toss their butts wherever they might fall.

I confess I'm annoyed by smokers in the workplace who spend 10 minutes of every hour out in the parking lot puffing away on breaks their nonsmoking colleagues do not enjoy.

Basically I hate everything about cigarettes. So why am I so uncomfortable with the growing national jihad against smokers?

It might have something to do with the fact that cigarette smoking is legal. Unhealthy, dangerous, stupid, but legal nonetheless.

And yet we increasingly treat cigarettes as contraband and those who indulge in them as social pariahs.

Cities are lining up to ban smoking in public gathering places, including bars and taverns, where smoking and drinking often go hand in hand. The Philadelphia City Council is set to vote Thursday on a widespread smoking prohibition. Mayor Street said he'd like to see a nation-wide ban.

### Workplace Litmus Test

And perhaps most troubling of all, Montgomery County is exploring a policy that would bar the hiring of smokers for county jobs.

We allegedly live in a free country, and that means having the freedom to indulge in harmful behavior. People smoke and drink too much and eat greasy burgers instead of salads and lounge in front of the television instead of exercising. And they will die younger because of it. Their choice.

Do we really want to go down this road of regulating legal but unhealthy behavior? If you want to take away my french fries, you'll have to pry them out of my cold, dead hand.

No one should be forced to breathe secondhand smoke, and smoking bans in workplaces, stores, and government buildings make perfect sense.

But if a bunch of smokers want to sit in a smoke-filled bar and suck in one another's carbon monoxide over beer, shouldn't they have that right? I won't be there, but I respect their right to turn their lungs into tar pits.

Conversely, nonsmokers are free to choose smoke-free establishments to eat and drink. And the more they vote with their pocketbooks, the more clean-air joints will open.

Let the marketplace decide.

### Freedom to Choose

A pub near my home went smoke-free last year, not because government put a gun to its head but because the owner saw money to be made. He lost the chain-smoking drinkers and gained the bigger-spending wine-and-dinner crowd.

When the place reeked of smoke, I chose to stay away; now I'm a regular. Isn't that how it should work?

Montgomery County thinks it can save on health-care costs if it refuses to hire smokers. But wouldn't it make more sense to simply charge smoking employees a higher premium for health insurance? If they want to smoke, fine, but let them pay their way. If you have ever tried to buy life insurance, you know the stiff premiums smokers face. Fair enough.

What Montgomery County, or any employer, should really be concerned about is finding the best possible employee. Do you turn down a hard worker with a sterling resume and references because he smokes? Do you hire a nonsmoking slacker instead?

If cigarettes are really that harmful—and we all know they are—let's outlaw them. That might, after all, actually send an unmuddied message to our children about what we really think of these cancer sticks.

That, of course, will never happen, not so long as the tobacco industry has Congress eating out of its hand.

Before we start placing smokers in the public stocks, we might want to take a second look at that $10 billion (yes, billion) buyout Congress approved for tobacco growers last fall.

Isn't it all just a little hypocritical?

*March 18, 2005*

## The Nonsense Logic of Angry Smokers

The smokers are restless.

Agitated, defensive, defiant, at times shrill, definitely ticked off. Their habit is under assault from all directions.

The Philadelphia City Council yesterday tabled a vote to join a growing list of cities around the country that have banned smoking in public places, including that onetime smoker's haven, the corner tappy. Montgomery County wants to save on health insurance costs by refusing to hire smokers. And in New Jersey, lawmakers are advancing their own smoking crackdown.

Like any cornered animal, smokers are lashing out. I know. I've been getting an earful.

Take, for example, the message left on my voice mail by Angry Smoker No. 1. She wants us to know tobacco for her is not a mere vice but a professional necessity. "Tobacco relaxes the nerves," she said. "It is something as an artist and a blues singer that I require for my job. I require a raspy voice; I require the effects of nicotine after each sculpture and painting."

Doesn't prefer it, mind you. Positively requires it. Just like the bottled oxygen she someday will be requiring.

Angry Smoker No. 1 argues that banning smoking in public places is just the start of a downward spiral into "prejudice and Nazism and fascism."

As she predicts: "OK, anyone 150 pounds overweight can't go into any restaurants; they're too fat and risk a heart attack. Also, all people who eat chocolate should be condemned because they're causing cavities and diabetes. And we should ban sugar. No sugar in coffee or tea!"

## Cry, Baby, Cry

And while we're at it, might I suggest we ban whining crybabies?

Somehow, in her nicotine-addled brain, all bad habits are equal. Chewing fingernails or mainlining heroin, it doesn't matter.

Then came Angry Smoker No. 2: "All children should be refused food if they are obese. All children who are obese should not be fed in the lunchroom. They are a health risk and insurance will go up for them."

And angry Smoker No. 3: "I think we should outlaw everyone who eats tuna fish, because the secondhand fumes from tuna cause ill health effects and make people throw up."

Cough . . . hack . . . wheeze.

Secondhand smoke, secondhand food odors—no difference at all. Not a bit. Same health risks, same watery eyes, same stench in your hair and clothes at the end of the day.

Not all smokers are this delusional. Several I heard from said they try hard to be considerate and only smoke where they won't bother others. Others told me they are not proud of their ways, but they reminded me it is a powerful addiction.

I know many smokers who indeed are trying to quit and are very considerate—so considerate, in fact, I sometimes forget they are smokers at all.

They just want to be left to puff in peace. Is that so bad? As I wrote Monday, I hate the smoke but love the smoker. I say if smokers want to crowd together in bars to inhale each others' soot, that should be their prerogative.

## A Little Honesty, Please

But I also expect smokers to be honest with themselves and everyone else.

When you insist on smoking in a closed car with your three kids buckled beside you, forced to suck your fumes, don't ask for our sympathy.

When you light up in a "smoking section" that is feet from the "nonsmoking section" with nothing but an imaginary line separating the two, know you are ruining someone's meal.

When you toss your butts out your car windows, know you are a pig.

When you stand in the doorway of a smoke-free building to get your fix, know you are making the rest of us run a foul gauntlet.

When you sneak a few quick puffs in the office restroom, know that we know. Hours later, we still know.

When you ask, "Mind if I smoke?" even as you're striking the match, realize that most of us will say "no" out of politeness but mean "yes."

There are many considerate smokers out there. They are not the problem. It's the inconsiderate ones, willfully blind to the effect their habit has on others, who have forced the issue and brought this whole national backlash upon themselves.

Puff on that, angry smokers.

*May 9, 2005*

## A Shared Concern for a Jane Doe

Jane Doe is nameless no more.

She died, homeless and unmissed, one year ago this week after a van accidentally backed into her in a parking lot in downtown Allentown.

Her lice-infested clothes were burned, her body laid unceremoniously in a pauper's field just off Interstate 78 in the shadow of a concrete plant. A small laminated card on a metal stake was her only headstone: "Jane Doe, May 12, 2004, County of Lehigh."

And she likely would have forever remained unidentified if not for two women who had never met but who both showed kindness to a lost soul haunted by mental illness.

Suzanne Kratzer, a retired eighth-grade teacher in Allentown, and Phyllis Graham, a retired nurse in Plymouth Meeting, stumbled into each other's lives after Jane Doe's death and pieced together the clues that would solve the mystery.

The clues stretched back a half century to when Graham was in nursing school at the former Germantown Hospital in Philadelphia. Her roommate and close friend for three years was a petite brunette from the town of Mount Carmel in the Poconos.

Her name: Leona Kovalick.

"She was just really a cute kid," Graham remembered, "bubbly, effervescent, fun-loving, carefree."

### Carefree Days

The two double-dated and spent summer Saturdays on the beach in Ocean City. "We had tons of fun, but she never would talk about her background," Graham said.

Graham was married in 1950, and her old roommate attended. "That was the last time I ever saw her," she said.

But Graham occasionally received letters from Kovalick, and as the years passed she could tell her old friend was becoming something beyond eccentric. Kovalick was always vague about where she lived and rebuffed Graham's efforts to visit her.

Enter Kratzer, the retired teacher who, while walking her dog near her home one evening in 2002, spotted a tiny, weathered woman lying on the porch of an office building, a large bag of clothing beside her. "I walked up and asked her if she was all right," Kratzer recalled. "It was nearly dark, and I was concerned for her safety. I asked if she'd had any dinner."

Kratzer would later return with a plate of food. She began aiding the homeless woman she knew as Lee, helping her secure widow's benefits through the Department of Veterans Affairs and trying unsuccessfully to persuade her to check into a shelter.

She also let the woman use her mailing address to receive letters.

After the woman disappeared off the streets in April 2004, Kratzer opened a card that had arrived for Leona Kovalick. It was from Graham.

## A String of Clues

The two women compared notes. They had both read about the unidentified Jane Doe: Kratzer in her local paper; Graham in this column. The more they talked, the more certain they were of Jane Doe's identity.

Graham remembered that Kovalick had told her she had a nephew in Louisiana. Graham located him, and he contacted the Lehigh County Coroner's office, which sent him a photograph of the unidentified woman.

"I immediately knew it was her," J. Richard Kanuch, a lawyer in New Orleans, said. An old X-ray from an arm fracture Kanuch remembered his aunt suffering provided a positive match, said Paul Zondlo, Lehigh County's chief deputy coroner.

Kanuch said his aunt had grown erratic and irascible by the time she was in her 30s. She could be sweet one moment and hostile the next. Her hygiene had become poor, and she could be physically abusive, he said. One by one, she alienated all 12 of her siblings. Eventually, she just vanished.

"I don't know what happened to her," he said. "She went through college; she did very well in nursing, dated several surgeons. . . . It's a sad story."

At noon Thursday, on the first anniversary of her death, the woman once known as Jane Doe will get a proper send-off. Kratzer, Graham, and a handful of Graham's nursing-school classmates will gather graveside.

A priest will say a few words. There will be flowers and a real headstone inscribed with a real name:

Leona Kovalick Bosker, June 1, 1928, to May 12, 2004.

⌐⌐⌐⌐⌐⌐ *May 13, 2005*

## A Friend Lost in Life, but Found in Death

Phyllis Graham stood by the small headstone in a pauper's field a few miles outside Allentown yesterday and opened the leather-bound yearbook from Germantown Hospital's Class of 1948.

Five of her nursing-school classmates from that year, all long retired, gathered around to see.

"There she is," Graham said, pointing to a black-and-white photograph of an attractive, petite woman in a white uniform, her chin upturned slightly. "That's Lee."

Leona Kovalick Bosker. She was born June 1, 1928, and grew up in Pennsylvania coal country. She died one year ago yesterday, an unidentified, lice-infested homeless woman crushed by a van as she huddled in a parking space.

What a long, sad journey it was.

As the yearbook playfully described her: "Here she is, the 'Blonde Bomber' of our class. She loves clothes and can really do them justice. Lee is the life of every party and possesses a certain personal charm that can't be beaten and a laugh that can't be mistaken."

The yearbook entry for Bosker concludes: "We know we need not wish her luck because it's already headed her way." But nothing resembling luck graced the life of this woman whose once bright future plummeted into the depths of self-destructive mental illness.

The women arrived at the indigent cemetery just before noon with a potted geranium and a bouquet of lilies-of-the-valley to place by their former classmate's grave. They wanted to give her a proper send-off. They wanted to remember her as what she once had been, not as what she had become.

"I couldn't bear to see her go that way," Graham said. "None of us wanted to see her buried like that."

Buried alone and unmissed in a pressboard box, a nameless, faceless vagrant designated by Lehigh County authorities simply as Jane Doe. The woman with no name.

It took the better part of a year, but Graham and a retired Allentown schoolteacher, Suzanne Kratzer, who had befriended the homeless woman on the streets of Allentown in 2002, pieced together the clues that allowed authorities to positively identify the former nurse.

Now her old classmates, who had not seen Bosker in more than half a century, gathered to say goodbye.

"She was a fun-loving kid, happy-go-lucky," recalled Audrey Raby of Bethlehem.

"Very outgoing, fun to be with," added Betty Salevsky of New Hope.

Graham recalled giggling with Lee late into the night in their dormitory—and losing their privileges because of it. She talked of sneaking out for ice cream, window shopping along Germantown Avenue, double-dating, and returning sunburned from beach trips.

Madeleine Bowen of Willow Grove said Leona could make her classmates laugh. She remembered one incident in particular. Tea enemas were sometimes used in those days to help sick children, and the first time Leona was ordered to administer one, she looked up and asked: "Do I put sugar and lemon in it?"

"All the girls howled about that," Bowen said. "She was serious. That's what was so funny about it."

All the women agreed they never saw any signs to make them suspect their former classmate's life could possibly one day come so unraveled. And yet it did. An utterly ordinary life come utterly undone.

Soon, a priest arrived. The group had invited him, because Bosker had been raised Catholic. The Rev. Harold Dagle, pastor of Immaculate Conception Church in Allentown, stood beneath the wind-whipped sky and told the small group that this woman was one of the many lost souls we pass on the streets every day. "And yet, somehow in death," he added, "she was found."

The priest prayed, "Eternal rest grant unto her, O Lord, and perpetual light shine upon her."

The women, standing in a circle clutching their flowers and photographs and memories, responded: "Amen."

Then Graham, her voice choking, said, "We had three years together—laughed a lot, cried a lot, but cared a lot about each other, too. Goodbye, Lee."

*June 7, 2005*

## Honked Off by Bumper Sticker

It was one of those days on the Pennsylvania Turnpike. Hot, muggy, crowded—and then came the dreaded red sea of brake lights.

My morning commute had barely begun yesterday when a Turnpike Commission truck with a flashing sign announced the bad news: "Prepare to stop. Accident ahead." Far ahead.

Traffic screeched to a standstill; twin ribbons of stopped cars stretched to the horizon, as if I had stumbled into the world's largest parallel-parking competition. There we sat, my fellow commuters and I, baking in the sun, our dress shirts wilting, out blood pressure rising. Together, we formed a sea of hot and bothered humanity, all late.

It was into this cauldron that Mr. Cheerful merged in his white SUV. He nudged his way in front of me, and that's when I saw it—a bumper sticker affixed prominently to the vehicle's rear window, right at eye level.

And what was his cheery message to his fellow road warriors?

Was it "Have a nice day"?

Was it "If you're happy and you know it, beep your horn"?

Was it "We're all in this together"?

Not even close. His bumper sticker read: "I want to kill you."

Great. I'm trapped on a slab of smoldering pavement, my gas needle edging toward E, the sweat trickling between my shoulder blades—and this Einstein wants to kill me. Just the pick-me-up I was looking for on this swell Monday morning.

### Mutual Contempt

"Want to kill me?" I muttered. "Not as bad as I want to kill you, pal."

Actually, I used a word considerably more colorful than pal. What can I say? Incivility breeds incivility.

Through the back window, I could see him jawboning on his cell phone, free hand drumming the steering wheel. This was not a high school kid trying to get attention; not a college-age student with a warped sense of humor. The guy was old enough to know better.

I want to kill you. What kind of public statement was that?

Did he think he was being funny? Provocative? Outrageous?

Given the message's position at eye level and its small type, I guessed it was aimed at tailgaters. Some of those slogans can be a hoot, like the one that goes: "If you can read this, you are within firing range."

That's witty. "I want to kill you" is only creepy and sociopathic. And with the number of road-rage assaults and homicides ticking ever upward, it's just a little chilling.

I wonder whether Douglas Heavlow, now in prison, sported one of those signs in his pickup truck the day in 2000 he intentionally sideswiped a car he thought was going too slow on the turnpike's Northeast Extension, killing a 21-year-old woman.

Or the enraged trucker on Route 22 in Northampton County, sent to prison for intentionally ramming his rig into the back of another vehicle, killing two men.

### Part of the Problem

Or the guy who fatally stabbed another man with a sword during a road-rage confrontation in Camden. Or the countless hotheads who have pointed, even fired, guns at other drivers.

I want to kill you.

Too often, the threat is real.

I had more than a half hour to sit, contemplating Mr. Cheerful's homicidal proclamation, and here is what I finally decided I would like to tell him:

Listen, buddy, no one is laughing. When you treat me with respect and dignity, I'll treat you the same. When you're considerate, I'll be considerate. When you open your arms to me as a fellow sufferer in the commuter wars, I'll embrace you back.

But when you tell me, and everyone around me, how little you value our lives, please know that you are something worse than just a coarse and crude (and not very original) cretin. You, Mr. Cheerful, are part of the problem. You are the abrasive that has turned society so rough and ugly.

In the battle between incivility and decency, between goonishness and gentleness, between those who build community and those who tear it apart, you are the enemy.

So do Greater Philadelphia a favor. Take your little bumper sticker, and . . . and . . . have a nice day, sir. Now, how hard was that?

*July 25, 2005*

## When Our Fears Lead to Prejudices

The sin of prejudice paid me a little visit last week.

No, I'm not proud of myself.

I was visiting New York City and arrived at the Port Authority late in the afternoon to grab an express bus back to Pennsylvania. On my way into the terminal, I passed a knot of National Guardsmen in camouflage, automatic rifles slung over their shoulders. They chatted among themselves as the masses streamed by, many like myself toting packages and suitcases. It occurred to me that there was little they could do to stop someone whose bag just might hold a bomb.

The bus was nearly full. Just as it was about to pull out, a last-minute passenger clambered aboard carrying a large rectangular package wrapped in a black trash bag. He kept his eyes down and sat in the only remaining seat, directly in front of me.

I felt an immediate, visceral response to his presence. My heart began to race, my stomach to tighten. I could feel the blood coursing through my temples.

The man was young, probably 19 or 20, with short black hair and a closely trimmed beard. He appeared to be of Middle Eastern ancestry.

Oh God . . . a suicide bomber.

## Calculus of Terror

Instantly, I told myself I was being ridiculous—and horrible. I knew nothing about this stranger, who may have been a college student or engineer or son on his way home to visit his parents. All I knew was that he somehow, at least at this moment, reminded me ominously of the faces of the young Muslim men who had detonated bombs in London on July 7, killing themselves and 52 others.

The more I tried to dismiss the notion, the more unnerved I became. It all made perfect sense to me. He was traveling alone (yes, and so was I); he was gripping a large package with both hands. At least to my eyes, he appeared nervous, uncomfortable. It occurred to me only later that his discomfort might have had something to do with the fact that people like me were presuming him to be evil based solely on his heritage.

Still, the pieces fit. Young, Islamic (I presumed) man. Alone, gripping an odd, bulky package. On a crowded bus that in about three minutes would be deep inside the Lincoln Tunnel. At rush hour.

First London. Now, once again, New York. A one-two punch. Of course!

As the bus approached the tunnel entrance, an acid burn rose from my gut. Fear, the likes of which I had not experienced in years.

## An Unfair Assumption

I was less than three feet from him. If a bomb went off, I wouldn't have a chance, wouldn't even know it. One moment I would be wondering. The next I would be gone.

I glanced around. If any of the other passengers harbored similar misgivings, they weren't showing it. But then, neither was I.

I like to think of myself as open-minded. I like to think I judge individuals on their merits. Yet here I was, ready to sprint to the front of the bus and demand the driver let me off. And for what?

Was this any different from the white woman who panics when a black man steps onto an elevator with her? No, it was not. I was guilty. Guilty of prejudging. Of racial profiling. Of stereotyping.

I knew that. Still, the terror was real. As we descended into the tunnel, I squeezed my eyes shut. If a terrorist were aboard, this is where he would act. An eternity later, we emerged into sunlight. I've never been so happy to see New Jersey. The man was still sitting there, gripping his package. I began to relax, but then he opened the plastic bag and began fumbling inside. Another wave of dread. Another false alarm.

By the time I stepped off the bus at my stop, my would-be terrorist was asleep. It was now clear: He was just a guy going somewhere—no different from me. I stepped off the bus, whispering an apology only I could hear.

The terrorist assault on free societies has many, many victims. Not all of them are hit by shrapnel and flying nails.

Curse the terrorists for what they have done. Shame on me for what I have allowed them to do.

*October 4, 2005*

## A Terrorist? Moi? Twice Exonerated

I'm not the world's most imposing man, so when I was yanked out of line at Philadelphia International Airport Saturday for a special head-to-toe, full-terrorist-alert search, I must confess to mixed emotions.

Part of me was annoyed. I had a flight to catch; what was this all about? Did I look like a terrorist?

Part of me was impressed. The Transportation Safety Administration screeners were professional and courteous—

a definite step up from the private security drones they replaced after 9/11, most of whom left the impression they had just been recruited from the Burger King take-out window.

Part of me was relieved. If a middle-age dad like me could merit such scrutiny, what chance did a real terrorist have of getting through?

And part of me was—yes, I'll admit it—a little flattered. This might well have been the first time in my life that someone considered me a threat to anything. As the TSA screener ran his beeping scanner over me, I couldn't help standing a little taller. Wow, they think I just might be dangerous!

Something on my boarding pass had set them off, a dreaded four-digit code. As soon as I showed it to the first guard, he opened the gate and politely said, "Follow me, please." He walked me into a fenced corral and called out for a male scanner to pat me down. Gee, I didn't get a choice?

## Assume the Position

As he snapped on his latex gloves, the pat-down expert calmly explained what he was about to do. I kicked off my shoes and assumed the position on the two footprints glued to the floor, my arms out in a messianic pose. "Unbuckle your belt," he ordered. Yikes! The banjo theme music from *Deliverance* played in my head.

Officer Pat-Down ran his hands around my waist, back and sides and up and down each leg, skirting dangerously close to that off-limits zone my mother always told me was no one's business but my own.

He had me roll down the waistband of my jeans, as if I might be hiding a Kalashnikov in there, and worked it over like he was kneading dough.

Meanwhile, his female colleague had my carry-on luggage splayed open and was poking through my socks, underwear, and toiletries. All I could think was, Please, Lord, don't let my wife's pantyhose be in there.

It was not even 7 a.m., and I was getting felt up by one stranger while another was fluffing my boxer shorts. All while my fellow passengers filed past, gawking and no doubt wondering what dark secrets I must hold to merit such scrutiny.

The female screener rubbed a cloth pad over all surfaces of my luggage and belongings, inside and out, and then ran the pad through a sensor in search of trace amounts of explosives.

### "Follow Me, Please," Again?

Several minutes later, I was deemed no risk to anyone whatsoever—there's a news flash—and left to buckle up and gather my belongings.

One random search I can live with. This is part of our duty as Americans in the post–9/11 age, to put up with these small humiliations and curtailments on our freedom in the name of safety for all.

But the next day, as I approached the security checkpoint in Chicago to come home, I was greeted by the same polite "Will you follow me, please?" and subjected to the same top-to-bottom search of my body and belongings. What was going on?

I asked the screener, and he had no idea. Many things could trigger a search, he said. Had I paid cash for my ticket? Bought it at the last minute? Was it only one-way? None of the above. "Or it might just be random," the screener told me.

Twice in two days?

I thought about blaming my travel agent. It was my first time using her, and I pictured her adding an addendum to my ticket purchase: "I'd keep an eye on this creep if I were you."

Perhaps it had something to do with the fact that my ticket was paid by a third party—my book publisher—and involved such a short stay.

What I do know is this: If the automatic triggers that ensnared me twice in two days also pinpoint would-be terrorists, the hassle and humiliation are all worth it. I'll assume the position without complaint.

But that's a considerable if.

*December 6, 2005*

## Even Vicki Needs to Work on Image

I was sitting in the Granite Run Mall near Media Saturday, doing what married men everywhere do while their wives are off giving the Visa card a good, plastic-melting, pre-holiday workout.

I sat and stared at the Victoria's Secret mannequin.

Actually, she stared at me; I merely returned her un-blinking gaze.

Vicki, as I named her, was hard to miss. She stood right in the front window under bright lights, balancing precariously on spike heels, curly blonde hair cascading over her shoulders. She was tall enough to play in the NBA with legs as long and fluid as the Schuylkill. She was as close to naked as one can get in public without risking arrest.

Her wardrobe consisted of a hot-pink Santa hat with matching hot-pink bra and tiny, tiny, tiny panties.

"Good Lord, there's not enough there for a decent hanky," I started to say before realizing I was sounding like my grandmother again.

I suppose it's a sure sign of middle age when you begin channeling long-departed relatives. One day you're young and worldly and rolling your eyes at the insufferable things grown-ups say; the next you are shamelessly stealing all their best lines.

## Barbie, All Grown Up

I had to admit, Vicki was fetching, just like a life-size Barbie doll, only better. Her features were even more exaggerated, the mile-long legs, impossibly small waist, and swelling bosom. Vicki's hip bones jutted out beneath a flat, sunken stomach; her arms were like matchsticks. If this idealized female miraculously came to life, she'd need to be rushed to the anorexia ward of the nearest hospital.

And we wonder why so many teenage girls have eating disorders and self-esteem issues?

Still, women of all ages flocked into the store, picking over the tiny garments. It goes without saying that there was a major disconnect between the plaster beauty in the window and those drawn in by her.

The shoppers came in all shapes and sizes. They were round and pear-shaped, droopy and angular, tall and short. Most, to be honest, even the teens, were varying degrees of overweight, a reflection of today's overfed and under-exerted America. The few I spotted who looked wispy enough to actually get away with wearing the revealing outfits in the front window turned out to be middle-school age. Yikes!

Believe me, if there were a Victor's Secret in the mall with an idealized male hunk in the window, we men wouldn't hold up any better.

(I swear I could single-handedly put Speedo out of business with but one brief beach stroll in one of its stamp-size swimsuits.)

In other words, unlike the robo-model in the window, the shoppers in the mall Saturday were human.

And we humans, fueled on supersize fast foods and bucket-size soft drinks, are getting fatter by the hour. Not just the adults but the children, too. Childhood obesity has more than doubled over the last 25 years.

## Reality-Fantasy Chasm

And, for once, metropolitan Philadelphia is a leading cultural trendsetter. All hail the caloric cheesesteak!

What are we doing about it? Gawking at life-size fantasy dolls that hawk clothing nearly none among us could or should attempt to wear.

No matter. The marketers ever more relentlessly ratchet up the perfection standard, extolling wildly unrealistic virtues of beauty. Each day, the chasm between reality and fantasy grows. As we grow pudgier, the models in the display cases grow slinkier. At this rate, it's just a matter of time before the malnourished mannequins seize control and begin sucking the nutrients out of us, which might not be such a bad thing.

As I sat taking in the crazed mall scene, I decided we should all work on one collective New Year's resolution. All of us should vow to eat better and exercise more, to curb the empty calories and get up off the couch and actually live a little.

While we're doing that, for better health and longer lives, we should all let our daughters know that they don't need to be cartoonish toothpicks to be valued in our thin-obsessed culture.

No offense, Vicki, but you could really stand to put on a few pounds.

*December 9, 2005*

## When Music Died, Words Were Born

Do you remember what you were doing when John Lennon was shot? I don't, but I do remember, with a searing clarity, the moment 25 years ago this morning when I belatedly heard the news.

I was a year out of college and working as a copy editor at a lackluster little newspaper in western Michigan. Because the paper was published in the afternoon, my shift began at an ungodly 4:45 a.m. My job was to clean up the copy of others—the best I could often hope for was to nudge the truly awful up to merely mediocre—and then put a headline on it.

On December 8, 1980, I went to bed early without turning on the television or radio, clueless about the seismic shock waves emanating from the west side of Central Park in New York. The next morning I walked into the newsroom unaware, and the other copy editors—older men who reveled in pushing my buttons—gleefully awaited me, Associated Press copy in hand.

"Your little hero Johnny Lennon bit the big one last night," one of them, a washed-up back-bencher named Brandon, said.

I literally reeled backward. I stuttered and stumbled. "He what?" I asked, trying to process it. They all found this immensely amusing.

I walked to the empty sports department and called my older brother in New York, waking him. "Did you hear?" I asked.

### No Words Needed

He had, the night before as he walked home from work through Central Park, and he had joined thousands of others in the impromptu vigil outside the former Beatle's apartment building. We just sat there on the phone, not saying much, not needing to.

Other icons of our age had "bit the big one," as Brandon would say—Elvis, Jimi, Janis, Morrison—and yet this was different.

The others had died of their own excesses. Lennon, publicly and painfully, had worked through his, finding peace in the simple joys of fatherhood. And he was killed by one of us, a deranged fan carrying a copy of J. D. Salinger's *The Catcher in the Rye.*

If the Beatles provided the soundtrack for my youth, J. D. Salinger provided the written text. Holden Caulfield— crazy, pitiable, confused, unpredictable Holden—was a little bit of all of us from that time, just as was Lennon, struggling to find his way, wearing his anguish on his sleeve.

And these two towering cultural icons came crashing together outside the Dakota apartments in a way that no one anticipated. Instant karma's gonna get you. . . . And yet, not like this.

The fact that his death came just one day after the anniversary of another generation's cultural earthquake— Pearl Harbor—only intensified the feeling that this was something far more than just a celebrity murder.

### Inside Treatment

Back at the copy desk, the news chief, a World War II veteran who as a 19-year-old had dropped bombs on Berlin, had relegated Lennon's death to two paragraphs on an inside page.

"You're kidding," I said.

Two hours later, the paper's editor, a no-nonsense veteran who had survived the bombing of Pearl Harbor, arrived. He glanced over the news budget, stopping at the Lennon story, slated for the "In Brief" roundup.

He looked at me, and for the first time sought my opinion. "This is big, isn't it?" he asked.

"It's really big," I told him.

He seemed to grasp what my coworkers could not: that, like Pearl Harbor, this event was about to shut the door forever on a generation's blissful naïveté and innocence.

All you need is love. . . . Right.

We ripped up the front page that morning and stripped the Lennon story across the top. Then my editor, this relic from a simpler time when good and evil were more clearly defined, turned to me and asked if I would write a first-person commentary on how Lennon's death affected me.

It was the first column of my life, and when I had completed it, I knew this was what I was meant to do.

In the crazy snowball of unanticipated circumstance that is life, four shots on a New York City sidewalk reverberated outward, touching many of us in unique ways.

For me that day, something inside died. And something was born.

⌒ *January 6, 2006*

## You've Got Spam
### *AOL's Trial CDs*

As I hauled the fifth bulging bag of trash to the curb after the holidays, I knew I had finally had enough.

The packaging that comes with nearly every purchase in this country, be it fast food or appliances or underwear, was totally out of hand. Do we really need that pint-size action figure double-boxed and shrink-wrapped and bound to a cardboard slab with nylon straps? Are we worried he'll escape?

Do we think those zucchini will somehow taste better sold on a foam tray and wrapped in enough cellophane to cover the Wachovia Center?

I had recycled as much paper and plastic as I could, and still my family of five was contributing mounds to the landfill—most of it useless packaging that came into our house with gifts and immediately went into the trash. It was obscene.

That's when I spotted the enemy. In the top of an open trash can, waiting to join the parade of flotsam on the curb, sat two unopened, plastic-wrapped boxes that had appeared in my mailbox days earlier like so many uninvited packages before them.

If an old flame were mailing me unwanted items, I'd be filing a stalker complaint with the local police. But these weren't from an old flame.

They were from America Online.

One was addressed to me by name, the other to "Current Resident." Both contained identical materials: shiny new CDs and an offer to "Try AOL 90 days risk-free!"

### An Uninvited Guest

The only problem was I didn't want to try AOL, risk-free or not. I'd been there, done that, and moved on to another Internet service provider years earlier. And yet, with the regularity of rainfall, the unwanted CDs showered in. As soon as they would arrive, I would drop them in the trash.

Maybe it was the postholiday grumpies, but I said out loud, "Not this time." I pulled the two AOL boxes out of the trash and scrawled in bold letters across them: "Refused! Return to sender." Man, it felt good.

The next morning, before dropping them in the mail, I decided to check with the post office. I explained I was fed up by these unsolicited mailings.

"It's trash," the clerk said. "Throw it away."

"But I don't want to throw them away," I said. I tried to tell her about the landfills and the packaging and the bags of trash, but she cut me off.

"We will not deliver it, sir."

I called a second post office and got the same answer. The bulk-rate postage used by AOL and other mass mailers does not include return service. "Unfortunately, you'll have to get rid of them yourself," the clerk said.

I scoured the AOL Web site, thinking it must have information on how to return these unwanted disks at the company's expense. I clicked on "Discover All Things AOL" and discovered everything except how to give the cursed things back. I clicked on "spam" (after all, wasn't that what this was?), but again no luck.

### Headed for the Trash

In my Internet searching, I discovered a group (www .nomoreaolcds.com) dedicated to ending the wasteful practice of sending out millions of unsolicited CDs, many of which will end up in the trash. The California-based group is collecting unwanted AOL CDs, and when it has gathered one million, it plans to truck them to the company's headquarters in Virginia and dump them on the front steps. I want to be there for that.

I contemplated mailing the CDs back to AOL (22000 AOL Way, Dulles, VA 20166). But why should I pay to return something I never asked for?

Finally, I found a toll-free number (1-800-466-5463) and quickly got through to a helpful AOL sales rep named Mike, who was eager to sign me up. When I told him I just wanted to be removed from the mailing list, he said, "Hold, please."

Of course, I was disconnected.

On my second call, after navigating a maze of automated prompts, I reached a polite man named Mbuso in South Africa. I never knew Pennsylvania could be pronounced so many ways. Mbuso took my information and promised that my days of receiving these ecological obscenities were behind me.

That still doesn't solve the problem of the two double-disk boxed sets cluttering my desk. Who knows, maybe I'll take up target shooting.

*February 17, 2006*

## With This Ring, Show Some Class

All right, men. We need to talk.

About The Ring.

Yes, that ring. The one Mario Mele, a former Mont-gomery County commissioner, gave to his then-sweet-heart, Janet Grace, last spring.

The ring that made a very big statement about love and devotion and lifelong commitment. A statement to the tune of two and one-third carats and $35,000.

The ring that Mele several weeks later wanted back after he decided that, you know what? Maybe marriage wasn't the best idea after all.

That ring.

Women, feel free to jump in here, but this really is a discussion we men need to have. And the question is this: Guys, when you give a girl a ring and then decide you've made a big mistake, what's the right course?

Not the legal course or the financially savvy course. The right course.

The honorable course.

As the whole nation now seems to know, the spurned bride-to-be did not return the mammoth mineral. Instead, she sold the princess-cut diamond, gave the money to charity, and kept the setting as a reminder, one guesses, of the hard knocks that can accompany even the biggest rocks.

Mele, 64, sued his 46-year-old ex-fiancée, demanding the full value of the ring, plus $100,000 for his trouble.

She dug in her heels. Ah, fickle love, from gauzy romance to embarrassingly public fights over the division of property before the first fistful of rice ever had a chance to fly.

## A Gentleman's Choice

The lawsuit was surging forward until this week, when national media attention suddenly put the fickle suitor and his jilted bride-to-be in the spotlight. She came off looking sympathetic; he came off looking, well . . .

A guy proposes and less than two months later un-proposes? He gives an extravagantly expensive piece of jewelry—and then asks for it back?

No man likes to look wishy-washy, and no man likes to look cheap. Mele was looking a lot like both.

With the national spotlight on them, the former love-birds quietly resolved the lawsuit this week. And they both lived happily ever . . . Oops, wait. Wrong ending.

And they both agreed not to disclose terms of the agreement. There we go.

We know what Pennsylvania case law says—that an en-gagement ring is considered a "conditional gift" that still belongs to the suitor until the moment the deal is sealed with a kiss on the wedding altar, at which time it becomes the property of the bride.

But what does the human heart say? Come on, men, help me out here. When you give a woman a ring, what's your intention? Are you really giving it to her, or just al-lowing her to hold your property on her finger until she coughs up her end of the bargain?

It's more than that? Or at least isn't it supposed to be?

## Rules of Engagement

If I were making the rules, they would come down to this: A gift is a gift, and givers don't take back what they have bestowed. Men, when you give a ring, the ring is hers.

Women, if you change your mind and dump your suitor in the dust before ever getting to the whole "till death do we part" part, at least have the decency to return the ring, even though you don't have to.

Men, if you are the ones doing the dumping, say goodbye not only to the no-longer Miss Right but also to the
large chunk of your savings that helped your local jeweler
send his children to really good colleges.

In the bigger scheme, the ring is chump change. Even a
$35,000 ring.

Here's the moral of the story:

If you need to ask for the return of your ring, you
spent too much for it.

If you need to wonder if she's worth it, she's not.

If you wake up one day after proposing with a pit in
your stomach, and you know—just know—that it's all
wrong, that this is not the person you want to spend the
rest of your life with, listen to your gut and be thankful
you're figuring it out now, not on your honeymoon.

If you're a gentleman, you will let her down as gently as
you know how.

You'll blame yourself.

You won't mention the ring.

You will know you're getting off cheaply, even without
getting it back.

*May 2, 2006*

# A Helping Hand, a Helping of Grace

After December's tsunami claimed countless thousands of
lives and left millions more homeless, many Americans
opened their checkbooks.

The Rev. Stanley Hagberg packed a sleeping bag, kissed his wife goodbye, and caught a flight into the heart of darkness.

For two months, Hagberg, a Conservative Baptist minister from Hatboro, slogged through muck and debris on the Indonesian island of Sumatra, helping in any way he could.

He carried sacks of rice, delivered cooking oil, shoveled mud out of homes, painted flood-stained classrooms. Mostly, he listened as grief-stricken villagers who had lost everything—their homes, their livelihoods, their children—bared their souls. "Everyone had a story to tell," said Hagberg, 66, who arrived back in Philadelphia last month.

The territory of Aceh on the northern tip of Sumatra, where he arrived February 7, was the closest landfall to the earthquake that spawned the tsunami that struck on December 26. A wall of water estimated at 100 feet tall slammed the western coastline, wiping out everything in its path. The official casualty count was 126,000 dead and 40,000 missing, but Hagberg said locals believe the numbers to be far higher.

"As far as the eye could see in all directions, it was just nothing but leveled foundations," he said last week from his office at the Normandy Farms Estates retirement community in Blue Bell, where he is chaplain.

## A Higher Calling

When the call had come asking him to join a Baptist relief mission to the devastated area, Hagberg hesitated.

He was no stranger to the country, having spent 16 years with his wife, Nancy, as Baptist missionaries in Indonesian Borneo.

But that was nearly a quarter-century ago. He wondered if he was still up to the rigors of such a job. "I was thinking of all the reasons I shouldn't go, but I realized it was just something God wanted me to do," he said.

Today, the minister believes the experience changed his life.

From the depths of one of the worst natural disasters in recorded history, he found a bright, shining light. It was the light of a shared humanity that transcended cultural and religious differences.

Aceh, the territory where he volunteered, is a stronghold of fundamentalist Islam. It is also a hotbed of a long-running rebel insurgency against the Indonesian government. Before the tsunami hit, Aceh was largely a closed society, suspicious of outsiders.

Enter the bespectacled and soft-spoken Hagberg, who kept his Christian beliefs to himself, knowing he was there to help, not proselytize.

A Conservative Baptist minister thrown together with fundamentalist Muslims in a ravaged and chaotic land? You might think this would be a recipe for a whole new level of seismic upheaval. But as Hagberg slogged through the mosquito-infested heat and humidity, he found just the opposite—something beyond beautiful, approaching the sublime.

## New Friendships

He came expecting suspicion; he left having found that most elusive state of grace—brotherhood blind to race, creed, or nationality.

"They were just very kind, loving, and affectionate," Hagberg said of the people whose lives he touched and who touched his. They were profoundly grateful to know an American traveled so far for no reason other than to hold out a helping hand.

"You really become part of each others' lives in that situation," he reflected. "Talk about feeling a person's pain. You want to weep with them for their loss, you really do."

One man told him, "You are a member of my family. You are my brother."

A local leader, overwhelmed with gratitude, offered to build a house for Hagberg so he could return with his wife to live in the man's village. "That, I think, is the greatest compliment I've ever been given," Hagberg said.

He took some lessons home with him. He knows now that actions speak louder than words, and that empathy is a gift returned many times over. He learned that in matters of life and death, differences melt away.

Through the jungle of despair, he glimpsed an elusive path—the one that leads to peace on Earth.

*August 7, 2006*

## Summer and Smoke

The year was 1967, and in the Summer of Love, as it would become known, the world seemed to be pulling apart from all directions.

Two of my cousins were fighting in Vietnam; the others were protesting the war in Ann Arbor. My older brother was growing his hair long; my mother was saying extra rosaries that she wouldn't lose him entirely.

Jimi Hendrix, Janis Joplin, and The Who stormed the country at Monterey, and the Beatles released *Sgt. Pepper's Lonely Hearts Club Band*, an album that filled our home all summer from the stereophonic record player with the flip-up turntable.

In my little world, it was the summer my best friend, John Rosser, and I set off to buy our first pack of cigarettes.

We were 10 years old.

As memory serves me, it was more Rosser's idea than mine, but I was a willing co-conspirator.

Many of the older kids in our neighborhood, which was nestled against a lake outside Detroit, were smoking. The young teens with their go-karts made with lawn-mower engines; the older teens with their souped-up Camaros and GTOs; the high-school girls we could only dream about, all blonde and bronzed, who worshiped the sun down at the neighborhood beach.

They smoked and looked beautiful. We wanted to, as well. So on a hazy hot morning we set off on our matching Schwinn Typhoon bicycles for the Sylvan Lanes Bowling Alley, several miles from our homes and well beyond the bounds of parental permission. Between us we had 35 cents—the exact price of one pack of cigarettes.

We chose the bowling alley because it had a vending machine in an outer foyer. We chose morning because we knew the place would be empty.

We were quaking with fear.

I played lookout, waiting with the bikes while Rosser went in. He returned seconds later to report he had gotten one dime in the machine before hearing a noise and fleeing.

It was my turn. I strolled in as nonchalantly as I could, my knees knocking, and pushed the quarter into the slot—then sprinted out as though a rottweiler were fast on my heels.

We stood together in the parking lot summoning our nerve. All that was left to do was select our brand—it had to be Marlboro; all the cool kids smoked Marlboro—and pull the knob. This time we went in together.

"You pull, I'll grab," Rosser said.

I spotted the Marlboro placard and pulled. The wrong knob.

Out came a pack of True cigarettes. Rosser could not have looked more horror-stricken had a rotting rat fallen from the machine. Oh no, girl cigarettes!

There was no time to lament. We could see adults inside.

"Let's go!" Rosser yelled, cramming the pack of Trues down the crotch of his shorts. We hopped on our bikes and pedaled off full speed, not stopping until we reached the vacant waterfront lot across from my house. There was nothing on it except a rickety stairway leading down a steep, wooded slope to the lake.

Near the water's edge was an oak tree with a hollow in its trunk—our stash spot for all sorts of juvenile contraband over the years. It was there we peeled off the cellophane, tugged open the foil wrapper and each placed one of the slim cigarettes between our lips.

Rosser struck the match, and we lit up. We must have looked ridiculous, puffing and coughing, our eyes watering, our heads spinning, our stomachs churning.

For being cool, smoking sure wasn't much fun. Nonetheless, we finished our cigarettes, then lit a third, passing it between us.

For good measure as we smoked, Rosser and I shouted every curse word we could think of into the treetops. Just for the thrill of it. Just to spite the Catholic nuns who taught us at Our Lady of Refuge up the street. We wanted them to know they hadn't won the indoctrination war yet.

How grown up it seemed, smoking and swearing in the very same breath. (Neither of us would go on to smoke as adults, though we both occasionally still swear at the treetops.)

Rosser and I buried the butts and stashed the cigarette pack in the tree hollow, then headed to my house, where we crept past my mother at the kitchen sink and locked ourselves in the bathroom to swish toothpaste in our mouths. We felt like soldiers after battle. With bluster and bravado, we laughed and jabbed each other at the sink.

We were 10 with no cares or worries in this troubled, confusing world. We were romping through the dog days of summer at full, blissful gallop. We had just conquered our first cigarette, as awful as it was.

It only made sense to celebrate by giving *Sgt. Pepper* another whirl before heading to the beach where the pretty girls with the burnished skin waited to ignore us once again.

# One Violent Summer,
# Two Worlds Collided

My uncle is an old man now, a retired priest who lives in a log cabin in the country and spends his days growing vegetables to give away.

But in the summer of 1967, he was the pastor of St. Catherine's Catholic Church, an inner-city parish in Detroit that was 40 minutes and a world away from the lakefront suburban neighborhood where I was growing up.

To his parishioners, he was Monsignor Vincent Howard. To his nieces and nephews he was simply Father Vin, an irrepressible practical joker who would greet you with a slap on the back—and drop an ice cube down your shirt. Or tell you to look out the window, then gleefully steal the cherry off your sundae.

On July 23 of that year, a Sunday night, my uncle was not joking. He was scared for his life.

Without warning, a large swath of Detroit had exploded in what would become one of the country's most violent race riots, a five-day conflagration that would claim 43 lives and entire blocks of the city. Stores were burning, firefighters were taking gunfire, the police were pinned down in their precinct houses—and my uncle was trying to protect his flock.

"The riot was going on all around us. That night I had 35 people staying in the rectory," he told me recently.

"They slept on the steps and on the floors. We couldn't raise our heads above the windowsills; we had to crawl because we were afraid we would get shot."

He was particularly worried about two families with young children whose homes were close to the violence. Early the next morning, he picked up the telephone.

"I called your mother and she welcomed them out there," he recalled.

That is where my memory begins.

I remember that morning, watching Detroit burn live on the television, and Father Vin's Chevrolet pulling into our driveway, loaded with children. Seven of them poured out, each holding a paper grocery sack of clothes.

As I recall, the youngest was about 8 and the oldest 15, a mix of boys and girls from two families.

Until that day, my world was my quiet neighborhood. It was swim lessons and horseback riding, Little League and touch football. I was 10 and had only the vaguest notion that places like Detroit, with their poverty and festering racial tensions, existed.

These kids, scared and visibly impoverished, were just as shocked by my world as I was by theirs. We considered ourselves middle class—one car, one black-and-white television—but I could tell they saw us as impossibly rich. We had a modern house on a park-like lot, and, down the street, a neighborhood beach and a dock with a sailboat tied to it.

In my suburban world, I had always thought I was pretty tough. I wasn't tough. These kids were tough. I was instantly intimidated. We eyed each other with awkwardness and suspicion.

My mother ordered everyone into bathing suits and down to the beach. Her purpose, I later would learn, was to have the opportunity to wash their clothes.

Only when we reached the water's edge did I realize that not all kids grow up with such a privilege. They stared nervously at the water in which I was so at ease. Not one of them knew how to swim.

The children stayed with us for five days while the riots raged to the beat of the Lovin' Spoonful's "Summer in the City" on the radio. The girls took over the bedroom and the boys slept in our tent-trailer in the backyard. My mom, her mother-hen instinct in overdrive, whipped up huge batches of hot-dog casserole and baked beans, and ordered her new adoptees, just like her own kids, to get in the tub and not come out until their feet were clean. At night, we roasted marshmallows and stared up at the stars, invisible to them in the city.

Gradually, we became friends. We rode bikes through the neighborhood together, ran through the woods and splashed in the water. I taught the boy closest to my age how to dog paddle, and he taught me how draw comic-book characters.

Day by day, hour by hour, we were figuring out that, for all our differences of place and privilege, we were not all that different.

In the end, we were all just kids. Kids who loved ice cream and hated baths. Kids who liked bare feet and dreaded the return to school. Kids who hid from chores and found mischief.

Through violent upheaval, our paths had crossed. Serendipitously, our separate worlds had come together, not with a crash but with a gasp of mutual awe.

For them, I imagine my life was a fairly tale, a tantalizing dream from which they soon enough would awaken. They had been plucked from their burning block and deposited here where all was safe and clean and well. They stayed just long enough to taste what lay beyond their grasp.

The greater lesson was mine to take. These children were my wake-up call. Never again could I so blithely take for granted all my parents had worked to provide. No longer could I presume that children grow up equal or that life is an even playing field.

On that last day, when it came time to say goodbye, we hugged and promised to write. Then they piled into Father Vin's Chevrolet and headed back to the smoldering ashes of their neighborhood. Their happy, gleaming faces smiled back at me as they disappeared into the distance.

*September 18, 2006*

## Talkin' 'Bout the Generations

The first time I saw The Who, I was a high school senior, and my lasting memory of that day was the terrifying sensation that I was about to be crushed.

It was December 1975 at the Silverdome in Pontiac, Michigan, a cavernous venue that was then home to the Detroit Lions. Tens of thousands of fans surrounded the place, waiting for the doors to open. General admission.

My best friend, Ray, and I had arrived early and were near the front. The crowd began to surge forward even though the gates remained locked. Tighter and tighter we were squeezed until I could not move my arms and could barely breathe. And then we were squeezed even tighter.

Just as panic began to sweep the crowd, the gates swung open and we poured forward, like flotsam in a raging river. It was a fitting start for a night of volatile, reckless rock-and-roll—music like I had never experienced before. Visceral, raging, ear-piercing, all cloaked in a haze of marijuana smoke.

The second time I saw The Who—the two surviving members, that is—was last week at the Wachovia Center. My, how we've all changed these last 31 years.

As my colleague Dan DeLuca noted in his review, the packed house was dominated by middle-age parents with their teenage children. Fathers and sons in matching Who T-shirts. Moms and daughters singing together, ". . . we won't get fooled again."

### A Family Affair

There were plenty of young adults in attendance, too—a testament to the intergenerational pull of this iconic rock band—but all around me the gathering had more the feel of soccer camp than a reunion of arguably the wildest bad boys of rock.

I did not detect a single whiff of marijuana.

My wife and I had brought our three children, ages 14, 12, and 9, Who fans all, to experience this cultural phenomenon before it was too late.

And by the end of the night, I acutely felt the push of time.

Pete Townshend, still hard-rocking, was grizzled. Roger Daltrey, that ethereal, blue-eyed pretty boy every high school girl once craved, was noticeably slower, his vocal range diminished, his microphone gymnastics a shadow of his earlier days. During one song, he missed his cue and apologized, "I can't hear the beat." Later he complained about being half-deaf.

It was like watching a pair of proud lions, the once un-challenged kings of their jungle, fighting back against their inevitable decline. They could still rock, no doubt about it, but there was a poignancy in their performance, an unspoken acknowledgement that their days of filling arenas and blasting out power chords were numbered.

In the men's room, a fan who appeared to be in his 50s said to my 12-year-old, "Remember this night, kid. The night you saw Pete Townshend and Roger Daltrey to-gether onstage." He knew what I knew: that the sun was setting on yet another icon of the '60s rock revolution.

### Passing the Baton

If they were not the same rock stars, I was no longer the same fan. I realized that as I watched drummer Zak Starkey, son of Beatles drummer Ringo Starr, come amaz-ingly close to capturing the frenetic majesty of The Who's original drummer, Keith Moon. I felt a swell of emotion in my chest. A father's emotion. I leaned over to my wife and said, "His dad must be so proud." And I meant it.

This was a rock concert, and I knew I should be, well, rocking. But I found myself glancing at my own children, their heads nodding to the music, and wondering where life's magical mystery tour might take them. Surely somewhere I could not even imagine.

The baton was passing from one generation to the next, from the lions to the cubs, from fathers to sons. The future was theirs now.

After the last song, the crowd gave the aging rockers the standing ovation they deserved, perhaps as much for what they were, what they will always be in our collective memory, as for what they are now.

Then Townshend darted off the stage with adolescent agility while his cohort hobbled off gingerly on what appeared to be arthritic knees.

As another graying rocker put it, rock-and-roll will never die. But its practitioners—those once eternally young gods of the stage—will indeed fade away.

*October 9, 2006*

## Dogged Writers in the Big House

So I'm at the White House having breakfast with the First Lady . . .

I know, it sounds like the opening line of a bad joke. But there I am on a recent Saturday, noshing on salmon and French toast beneath a giant portrait of Benjamin Franklin.

The closest I've ever been to power was in 1968 when I held the flag for the governor of Michigan. I'm pretty easily starstruck.

"Is this really happening?" I whispered to my wife.

She opened her blazer to show me the embossed paper hand towel she'd snatched from the powder room. "It's really happening," she answered.

I glanced at the marine guards in their dress uniforms and wondered what federal laws we were breaking.

Yes, we. I reached into my pocket and showed Jenny that I, too, had purloined a souvenir—a cocktail napkin stamped with the words: "Seal of the President of the United States."

"Guantanamo, here we come," I said.

For the record, Jenny and I weren't the only ones nabbing souvenirs. The word was out among the 150 or so breakfast guests that the presidential paper products were the hottest ticket in town.

We were all there for one simple reason: Many of us had written books. And Laura Bush, that former librarian, loves books.

She loves them so much that six years ago she launched the National Book Festival with the Library of Congress to bring authors and readers together to celebrate the written word.

Each year the festival has grown. And on that Saturday, 100,000 readers of all ages poured onto the National Mall to attend book readings and signings. If you fear the written word is on the verge of extinction, and that electronic gadgetry has eclipsed old-fashioned words on paper, the scene on the Mall would brighten your outlook.

The crowd included every imaginable demographic slice. But it was the young people who caught my eye. School children collecting autographs, high schoolers with pierced eyebrows, college students taking notes. One student told me she drove all the way from Amherst, Massachusetts.

The written word was boldly alive on the Mall that day, as big and brazenly virile as the Washington Monument itself.

But before the festival came the breakfast, and before the breakfast—the previous night—came a black-tie gala at the Library of Congress for the authors and sponsors, attended by President and Mrs. Bush, Secretary of State Condoleezza Rice and other administration officials.

"Hey," I said, spotting Attorney General Alberto Gonzales, at the next table. "It's the torture guy!"

But we weren't there to debate torture or unconstitutional detainments or the ever-bleaker quagmire in Iraq. We were here to agree on one thing: the value of words on paper.

The invited authors, poets, and illustrators covered the spectrum. Legal thriller writers Scott Turow and (Philly's own) Lisa Scottoline were on the program. So were investigative reporter Bob Woodward and Khaled Hosseini, author of the acclaimed *The Kite Runner*, as were Pulitzer Prize winners Doris Kearns Goodwin, Taylor Branch, and Geraldine Brooks.

Yeah, and bringing up the rear, me—that columnist who wrote about life with an insane Labrador retriever.

All invited by Mrs. Bush to send the message that books matter.

She thanked the writers "for the many solitary hours you spend working to enlighten and inform and inspire and entertain all the rest of us." When I had a few moments with her, I thanked her for championing some-thing that matters.

In the English language, it all comes down to this: Twenty-six letters, when combined correctly, can create magic. Twenty-six letters form the foundation of a free, informed society.

Whatever you think of the president and his adminis-tration—and, frankly I don't think much of them—let's give credit where credit is due.

Laura Bush is doing more to promote reading and liter-acy than any First Lady before her, and perhaps more than anyone in the country today. She is using her substantial bully pulpit to spotlight reading and literacy and to hook children—the next generation—as lifetime lovers of books.

The president's legacy might be in question; his wife's is secure.

Well done, Mrs. Bush.

And thanks for the cool napkins.

*October 13, 2006*

## A Searing Lesson in Forgiveness

In hindsight, I realize I was driving too fast, especially given the rain-slicked roads.

Ahead of me at an intersection, a car was stopped with its left blinker on. I bore down, expecting it to turn out of my path at any second.

But the car did not turn. By the time I hit the brakes it was too late. I skidded and slammed into its rear end, catapulting it into cross traffic.

Miraculously, the other vehicles all avoided the car, but I realized instantly my moment of poor judgment could easily have resulted in the death of an innocent stranger.

Across the intersection, we both pulled into a parking lot. The man inside looked like he could have been a bar bouncer, large and intimidating.

He wasn't hurt and neither was I. His car did not even have a dent where I hit it.

"Man, you almost got me creamed," the driver said.

I apologized profusely. He had every right to be angry, and I was braced for him to get in my face, poke a finger in my chest and dress me down with a string of obscenities. People had been beaten up, even shot, over lesser transgressions.

Then he did an amazing thing. The stranger shook my hand and said, "It was an accident. Don't worry about it."

## The F Word

That was years ago, but the moment has stuck with me because it put me on the receiving end of an important lesson. I had erred and he had forgiven.

Forgiveness.

We all want to think we are capable of it. And for most of us, most of the time, we are.

We can forgive a child who disobeys. Or a delivery driver who accidentally knocks over our mailbox. Perhaps even a thief who takes what is ours.

But what about an offense far worse? Unspeakably, unimaginably worse?

What about a stranger who barges into a country schoolhouse, lines up 10 innocent children against the chalkboard—and opens fire?

What parent, what community, could forgive that?

We now know the answer.

Within hours of Charles Carl Roberts IV's murderous assault on the Amish school in Lancaster County on October 2, the local Amish community was already expressing forgiveness.

Even before they had a chance to bury their dead daughters. Even as they huddled bedside as other victims clung to life by the most tenuous of threads. Complete and total forgiveness.

What was done was done, and the killer, too, was now dead. No amount of anger or vengeance-seeking would bring the children back or the killer to justice. The Amish had two choices: Descend the dark staircase into bitterness, or follow the tenets of their faith and rise above it. They believe all acts, even one as monstrous as this, are part of their God's inexplicable plan.

And so they forgave.

### Mercy Amid Grief

Amish neighbors went to the killer's home to console his wife and other relatives. They attended his funeral and invited his widow to attend at least one of the murdered girl's funerals. As thousands of dollars poured in from around the world to help the families of the victims, the Amish set up a fund for the killer's own children.

Unbelievable.

Unbelievable and somehow beautiful all at once.

It is the stuff sermons are built around. If the Amish can forgive such a ghastly violation, can't we all try to be just a little more forgiving of the slights and hurts and wrongs of daily life?

The simple people know what many of us still have not figured out, that the ever-escalating violence of vengeance has no end, and that the acid of revenge etches the human heart with deep and permanent scars.

Imagine if the ethic of unilateral forgiveness could envelop the Sunnis and Shiites in Iraq, the Catholics and Protestants in Ireland, the Jews and Palestinians in Israel. Imagine if it could permeate the streets of America, where rival gangs kill over colors and young men settle scores over respect with 9mm Glocks.

The Amish have found the road to a higher place. The rest of us could do worse than to be a little more like them.

*November 3, 2006*

## Flying's Fearful New Annoyances

It says something about my state of mind that I found myself on a flight from Pennsylvania to Texas last week counting the contents of my in-flight snack.

I dumped the bag onto the tray table and used the eraser end of a pencil to line up the contents in little rows.

My "premium blend" power snack consisted of exactly nine and a half soy nuts, five and a quarter sesame sticks, and five lonely mini-pretzels. Together, this gastronomic feast totaled a whopping one-half ounce.

*Bon appetit*, passengers!

Isn't it nice to know the airlines are doing their part to address the national obesity epidemic? I'm just grateful they didn't stick me with the "dieters' blend."

I don't normally spend my time obsessing over snack mixes, but this is what the sorry state of air travel in America has done to me. Turned me into a raving soybean counter.

Remember the good old days when fliers loved to hate the airline food? Back in those days of yore when there actually was airline food? Yes, I know. I'm giving away my age.

## Shoes Off, Please

The food is just a small part of it.

The joys of modern air travel now begin at the security check-in line where we line up like cattle, removing shoes and blazers, whipping off belts, clutching trousers to keep them from heading south.

No one wants to grumble about measures to keep the nation safe from terrorism, so we shuffle silently through in our stocking feet. But honestly, some of the security rules are plain dumb.

Somehow I don't feel any safer knowing that the grandma in front of me in line just had to throw out her four-ounce bottle of Oil of Olay.

Immediately after the liquid-explosive scare several weeks ago, anything liquid or gel had to go. Thousands of dollars worth of cosmetics and soft drinks were tossed out. The terrorists, I'm sure, were mightily amused.

Then the Transportation Security Administration tweaked the rules to allow travelers to carry whatever liquids and gels they could fit into a one-quart plastic bag, as long as no one item was more than three ounces.

I was in the security line a couple of weeks ago and the man in front of me had his toiletry kit boiled down to the bare essentials—tiny travel sizes of toothpaste, deodorant, and mouthwash. But he forgot the plastic bag.

The TSA inspector told him, no baggie, no go. The man dumped them in the trash. And for what?

When my turn came, I had my essentials in the baggie, having learned my lesson on a previous flight when all my liquids were confiscated.

But one of my items was a six-ounce toothpaste tube. "This container is too large," the TSA inspector said.

"But it's nearly empty," I told him. At best, it had an ounce left in it.

"Doesn't matter," he said. "We go by the container size, not the contents."

## Some Common Sense

I wanted to retort: "So it's OK to have six ounces of toothpaste in two three-ounce containers, but not one ounce in a six-ounce container?"

I knew where arguing would get me. "Whatever," I said and tossed it.

We need security, I realize that. We need rules. But a little common sense would be nice, too.

The overzealous security rules wouldn't be so bad if checking luggage was not such a crap shoot.

My son and I flew from Philadelphia to California for a long weekend a few months ago, and I did something I never do—checked our luggage. Big mistake. The bags didn't show up until we were nearly ready to return home.

Even when bags are not lost, the waits to retrieve them in baggage claim can exceed the flight time. Especially here in Philadelphia, home to the why-hurry-I'm-hourly school of customer service.

U.S. Airways' baggage delays and losses in Philadelphia have become so embarrassing, the airline's top brass went public with a plan to fix the problem. I'll believe it when I see it.

For the beleaguered passenger, the choices are bleak: Check your bag and pray you'll someday see it again, or carry it through security and face the toothpaste gestapo.

The only consolation is knowing, once you finally make your flight, a hearty half-ounce snack awaits you.

Just try not to spoil your appetite.

# Mortality Check
## Is in the Mail

The letter arrived unannounced at my home, hidden amid junk mail.

It came in a plain envelope with a simple street address on the back. There was no outward hint as to its contents, and for good reason. I would have promptly thrown it away.

Yes, it was that letter. The one no one wants to receive but all one day will. The letter that makes an IRS audit seem like a lottery prize.

The one that slaps you hard on the face and tells you once and for all that you never again will fit into those 30-inch-waist jeans.

"Dear Mr. John J. Grogan," it began.

I scanned the opening paragraph, picking out the operative phrases: "fully eligible . . . membership . . . benefits . . . life over 50."

Life. Over 50.

I began to pray. Oh, Lord, please, no. Not that. Anything but that.

For whom does the American Association of Retired Persons troll? It trolls for me.

My official AARP membership card, No. 1567627, was attached.

"Honey," I called to my wife. "Where's the bourbon?"

## Counting the Days

For the record, I am not 50. Not even close. Fifty remains a faraway speck on the horizon. I remain a proud member of the forty-something decade. Some of my best friends are thirty-somethings. A few are even fresh-faced twenty-somethings.

I still do ridiculously foolhardy things like teeter from a high ladder holding a chain saw.

I am not 50, OK? That's still four months, 10 days, and 17 hours away. Not that anyone is counting.

But could the AARP wait?

The letter tried to lure me in with a long list of "benefits and services" aimed at nascent geezers-in-waiting.

A safe-driving course, for starters. I couldn't help conjuring up a horrible premonition of me in a Buick Skylark tooling along at 43 mph in the high-speed lane of Interstate 95. Nooooo!

My membership comes with a magazine to remind me that I'm on the downhill slide to 100.

It offers regular updates on Social Security, an entitlement program I am perfectly happy never to qualify for.

I also can use my AARP card, and I quote, "to save on shoes."

All colors, or just white?

I won't deny it. The arrival of my AARP card threw me into a total funk. This was my parents' organization. Why was it bugging me?

I tried to put the best spin on it. Finally, those bushy eyebrows I've always craved would be coming into their own!

### The Eternal Paterno

But there was no denying the harsh reality. Life's best chapters may still lie ahead, but any way I spun it, the story line ended the same way.

At the cemetery.

That's when I thought about Joe Paterno. What better role model for the second half-century?

The Penn State coaching legend will turn 80 next month and still gets up every morning to go to work.

Saturday he was flattened by two players who crashed into him, breaking his leg, but not his intensity.

I loved the photo of Paterno being carted off the field with his injured leg up. His face, equal parts disgust and impatience, said it all: Get the damn leg fixed so I can get back to work, will ya?

Not that I harbor fantasies of coaching college ball. But when I grow up, I want to be like Jumpin' Joe Paterno.

Not a stubborn-as-a-mule coach. But someone who refuses to relent to the ravages of time. Someone who embraces his passion without compromise and won't let go. Someone who tells age what it can do with itself.

A guy who won't slow down.

My father was a bit like Paterno that way. He hurled himself at life full bore every day, right up to his last. I would have put him, at 89, up against men 20 years younger.

An automotive engineer, he liked to say, "The worst possible thing for a car is to let it sit and idle." The same rule applies to the human machine.

Bring it on, AARP. Bring on the membership cards and senior discounts.

Fifty may be right around the corner. But as a great coach might tell his players in the halftime pep talk of life: You're only as old as you let yourself be.

*November 24, 2006*

# Just Say No
# to Black Friday

Good morning, shoppers.

Today is the big day. The one that sends crazed bargain hunters into a salivating frenzy. The one that sends retailers and credit card companies into a heroin-like state of bliss. The one that sends anyone still clinging to the real meaning of Christmas into the dumps.

Yes, today is the appropriately named Black Friday. A dark and gloomy and cynical day.

Around our region, tens of thousands of shoppers will work off yesterday's big turkey dinner by rising before dawn, jostling for parking spaces, racing up and down aisles, lunging for the latest must-have toys and electronics, and waiting in long lines to pay.

Tempers will flare, heads will throb, feet will ache. But it will all be worth it because at the end of the day our cars will be filled with . . . stuff. Stuff to show our loved ones how much we care.

You wouldn't think we famously materialistic Americans would need our own special day to ratchet the spending orgy up. But that's what today is.

Actually, that's not quite accurate. Today actually began yesterday. That is, the Black Friday shopping kickoff actually got started at many stores on Thanksgiving afternoon or evening.

Why spend the holiday at home with your family when you can get a head start on the purchases that mean so much more?

### Finding Balance

It's hard, I know.

As parents, my wife and I struggle to find the right balance. In our minds, we're giving our children a nice assortment of gifts without going overboard. Then they compare notes with their friends, and I see the disappointment on their faces. That Monopoly game instantly loses its luster when Tommy up the street whizzes by on his new all-terrain four-wheeler.

The new meaning of Christmas comes down to this: guilt. To avoid it, we buy like there is no tomorrow. There's not much joy in it, but at least we've covered.

Baby Jesus would be so proud.

May I make a modest proposal?

Just say no.

Say no to the rat race.

Say no to the hype.

Say no to the notion, carefully planted by marketers and advertisers, that good parents who really care shower their children with obscene amounts of toys and gifts—even if they need to max out their credit cards to do it.

Look away from the light, my friends. Block out the white noise. Ignore the "only X shopping days left" pitches.

The season is not about buying junior 26 different toys, most of which will be obsolete, broken, or ignored within weeks. It's not about spending on steroids. At least it didn't start out that way. You don't need to be particularly religious to recognize that.

### Pricey Playthings

A teen in Allentown laid out $600 for the newly released and wildly hyped PlayStation 3—and minutes later was robbed of it at gunpoint.

I'm not sure which distresses me more: people robbing one another with guns, or Sony shaking down kids for a $600 toy that, mark my words, will be out-of-date in 24 months.

Last year, I wanted to give a special gift to a special friend who did a lot for me in the previous months. I bought into the hype, thinking I needed to spend several hundred dollars to convey the proper level of appreciation. In the end, I spent zero.

Instead, I holed up in my basement night after night and slowly crafted a simple keepsake box out of a black walnut log that came from the woods behind my house. I sawed the log into planks, planed the planks into boards, fitted the boards together, then sanded and varnished and polished.

I'm no master craftsman, and the final product reflected that. But my friend was touched by my efforts in a way no purchased gift could touch. The real gift, though, was to me.

I rediscovered the true joy of gift giving. A joy unburdened by guilt or pressure or competition.

Here's the secret: It's about giving of yourself.

Today I plan to observe Black Friday by sitting home in front of the fire with a good book. The mad march on the mall can be somebody else's crusade. Care to join me?

*December 11, 2006*

## An Army of One Takes on Litter

On any given morning in Roxborough, you might spot a middle-aged woman bundled against the cold, making her way along Ridge Avenue, stooping to retrieve anything she finds in her path.

You will know her because she will have a mixed-breed dog at her side, and, almost always, other people's discards in her hands.

She might stop to scoop up tossed fast food or a crumb-filled doughnut bag or a beer can with one last swill inside.

"If it's too disgusting I won't pick it up," she says. "If it's oozing or gooey, I won't touch it." Her name is Diane

Bones, and she wants you to know that she is not bag lady looking for her next meal. She is a gainfully employed homeowner and proud resident of the neighborhood who is waging a one-woman battle against what she considers Enemy No. 1: litter.

It's everywhere—blowing down the streets, covering the sidewalks and tiny yards, Bones says.

When she moved into the city from Media, shortly after getting married in 2000, she noticed it immediately. And it drove her crazy.

"I love living in the city," she says. "I love everything about it. My only complaint is the litter."

### Daily Good Deed

And so Bones, 53, took it upon herself to pick up the messes left by strangers. She has turned her morning power walk with Samantha, the shepherd mix, into a street-sprucing mission.

What does she snag on a typical walk?

"Soda cans, cigarette packs, candy wrappers, potato-chip bags, newspapers, milk jugs, beer and booze bottles," she says. "On our street, litter is just an accepted way of life. People just walk right by it."

Bones lives across from an Acme, and she often picks up discarded packaging from items customers have just bought. Plastic bags from the nearby Rite-Aid blow about.

A couple of doors from her home sits Levering Elementary School, which Bones says is a source of a lot of the trash. Children drop their wrappers and soft-drink bottles without seeming to realize they're littering, she says.

Her route takes her near Roxborough High School. She has watched students exit a nearby doughnut shop, dropping their trash as they walk.

Sometimes she confronts them. "I will literally yell across Ridge Avenue, 'Pick that up!'" she says. Usually they do.

"They look startled. They don't think they're doing anything wrong."

The culprits are not just children. She has caught plenty of adults in the act, too, including a neighbor who blithely tossed a worthless lottery ticket out the window of her car.

"She didn't win, so we all lose," Bones grouses.

## A Symbol of Surrender

What bugs her almost as much as the litterers are those who simply step over the trash, even if it is in their own yard or in front of their business.

She admits she's a bit obsessive about litter. She sees it as a cancer that eats away at civic pride and community fabric.

"Even through it seems like a minor problem, litter sets the tone for a we-don't-care attitude," Bones says. "It's symbolic of an apathy, a surrender. It's saying, 'You know what? I give up.'"

Bones is not about to give up.

When she moved in, there were no public trash cans near Levering Elementary, and neighbors told her that was just the way it was. She made one call to then-Councilman Michael Nutter, and two trash receptacles soon appeared outside the school.

One person's efforts really can make a difference.

Every morning, Bones picks up what she can, even as passersby stare, thinking she must be crazy or homeless or both. The next day, more trash always awaits her.

"Sometimes it does feel futile," she admits. "Some days, I ask why I even bother."

Still, she soldiers on.

"Have I made a difference? Who knows? I can't be responsible for the whole world, but I can be responsible for the little spot in front of my house.

"If my little corner of the world can look better, maybe it will start to snowball."